Emily's Book of Strange

BY **ROB REGER**

**ILLUSTRATED BY
BUZZ PARKER
AND ROB REGER**

CHRONICLE BOOKS
SAN FRANCISCO

art snobs
ILLUSTRATED BY BUZZ P~~ARKER AND ROB REGER WITH THE HELP OF BRIAN BROOKS, ADELE PEDERSON,~~
GRACE F~~ONTAINE, AND LEE TOM.~~ THANKS TO NOEL TO~~LENTINO, MATT REED, THE COSMIC CREW,~~
AND LUPA THE PUNK ROCK KITTY. my slaves
noTHANKS TO YOU!
WWW.EMILYSTRANGE.COM buy or die

LIBRARY OF CONGRESS CATALOGING-IN-PUBLICATION DATA AVAILABLE. who cares?

ISBN 0-8118-3986-9
MANUFACTURED IN ~~CHINA~~ strangeland
DISTRIBUTED IN CANADA BY RAINCOAST BOOKS ← hippies
9050 SHAUGHNESSY STREET
VANCOUVER, BRITISH COLUMBIA V6P 6E5

10 9 8 7 6 5 4 3 2 1

CHRONIC~~LE BOOKS LLC~~ ~~the~~ censors
85 SECOND STREET
SAN FRANCISCO, CALIFORNIA 94105
WWW.CHRONICLEBOOKS.COM

emily

follow the leader...

&

SEE
STRANGE

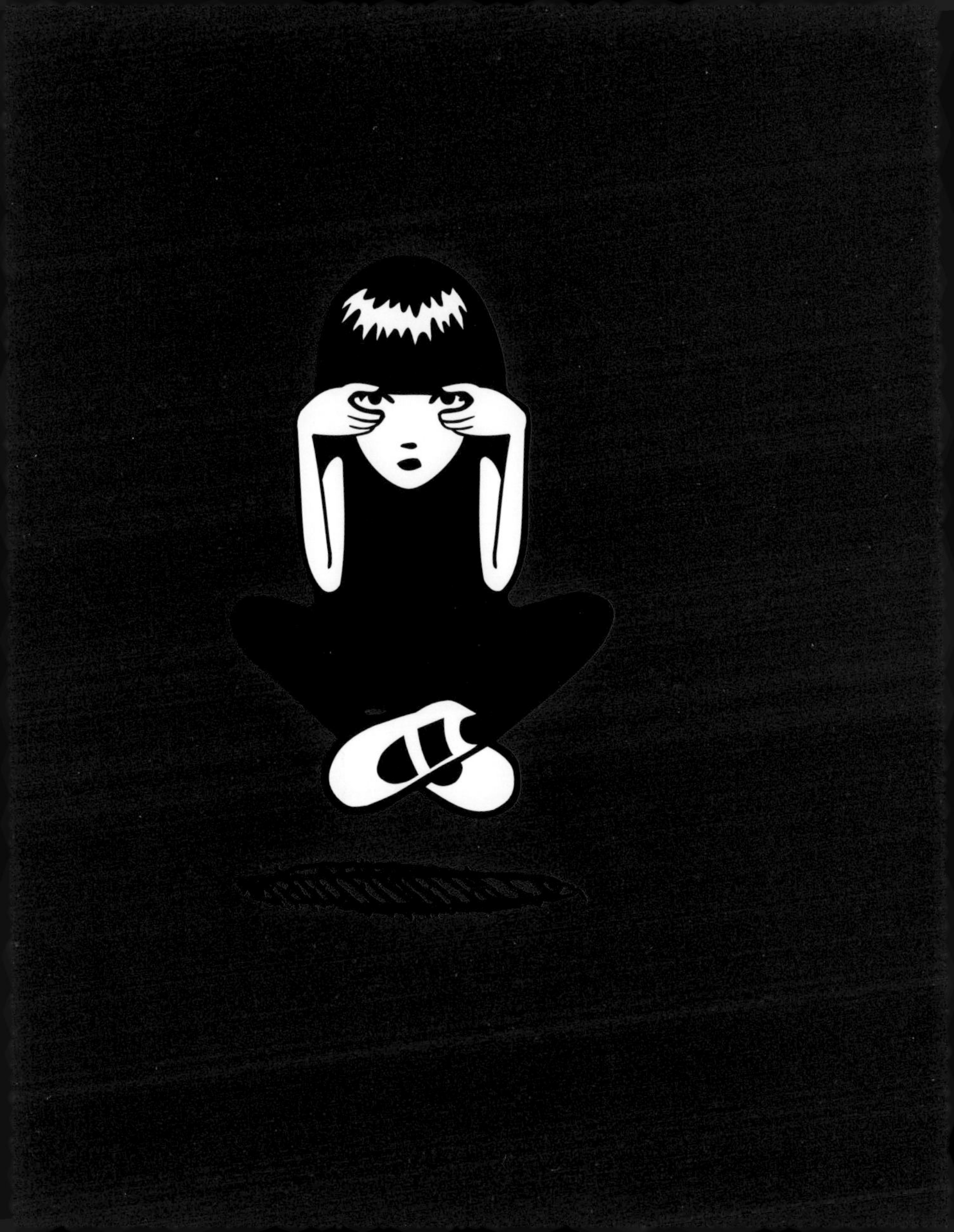

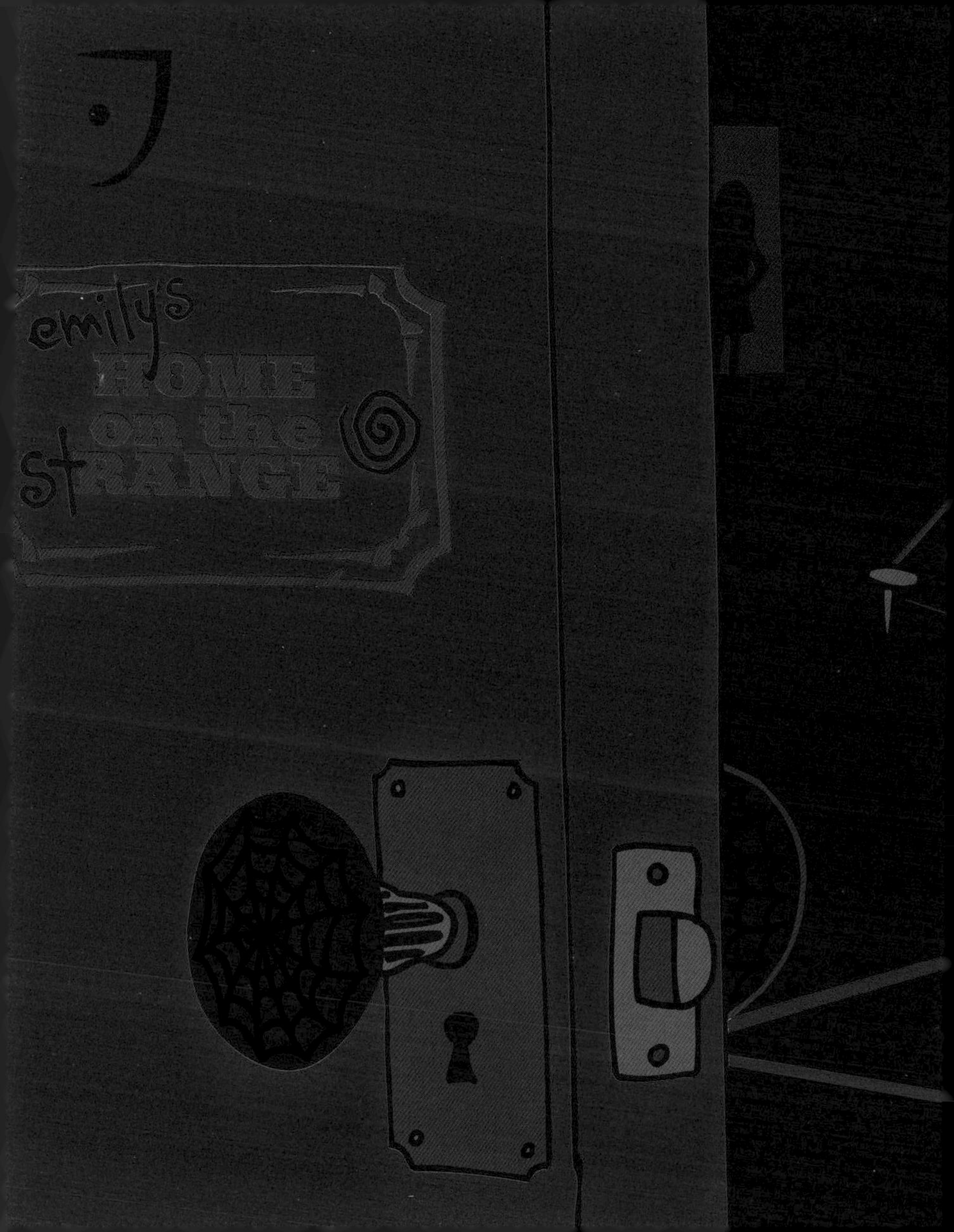
emily's
HOME
on the
STRANGE

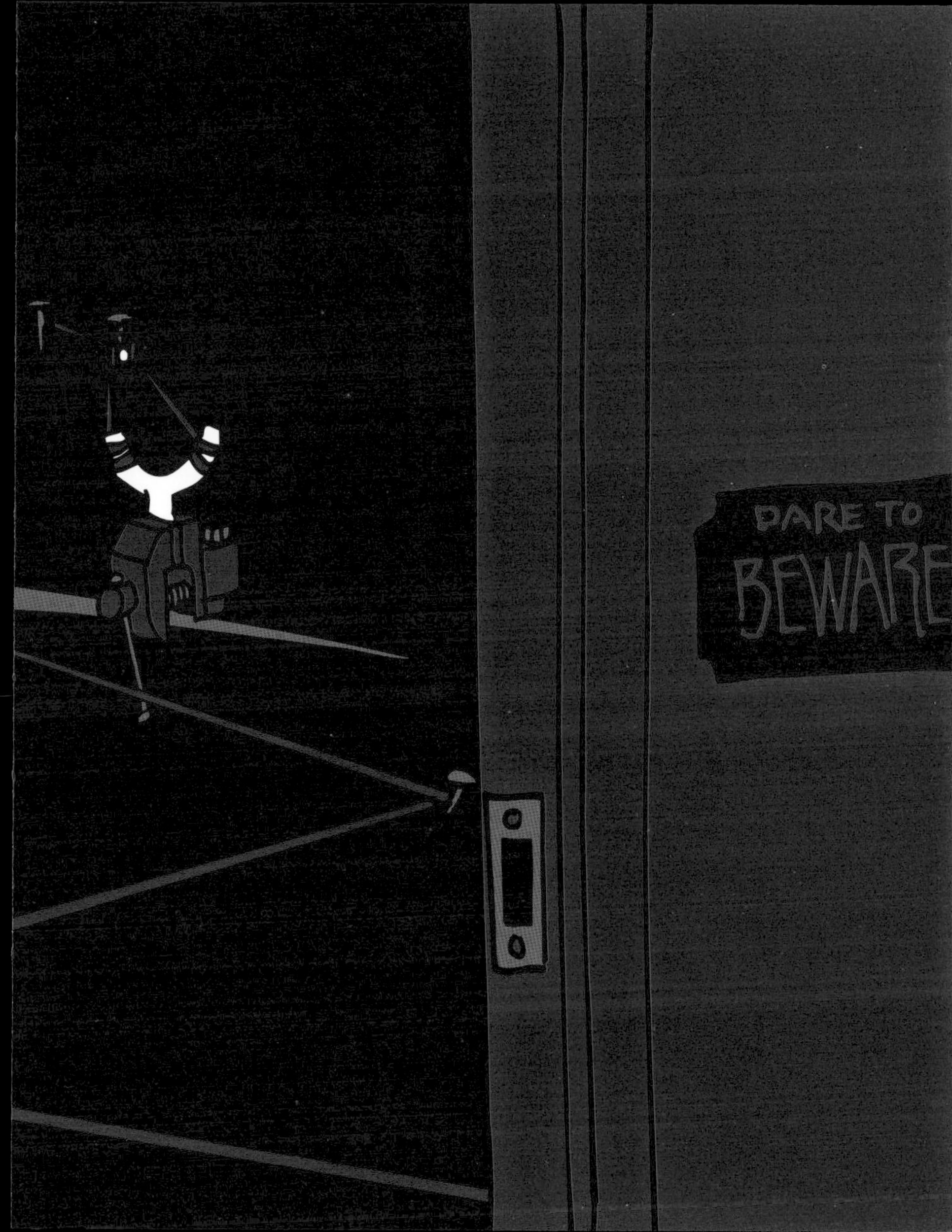
DARE TO
BEWARE

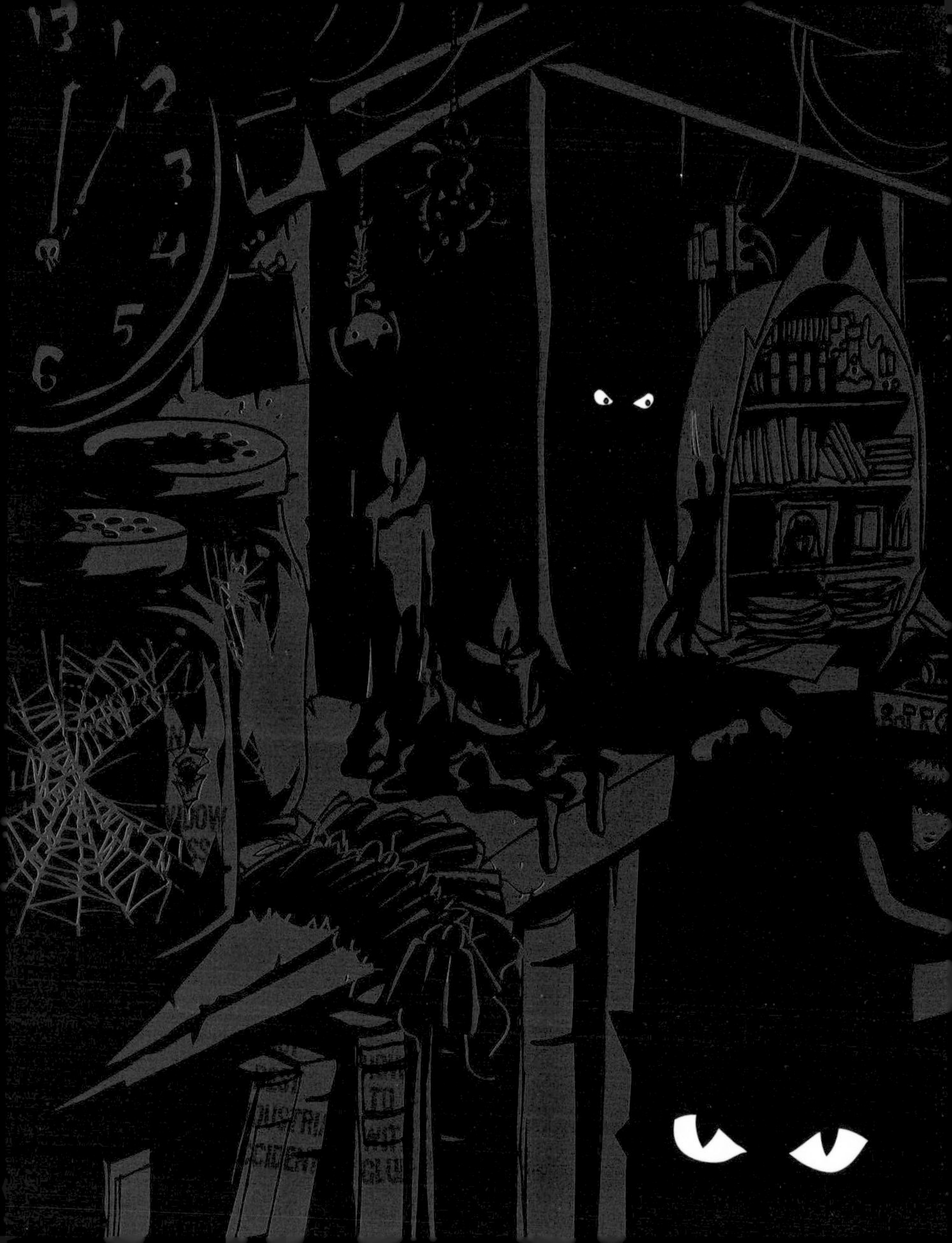

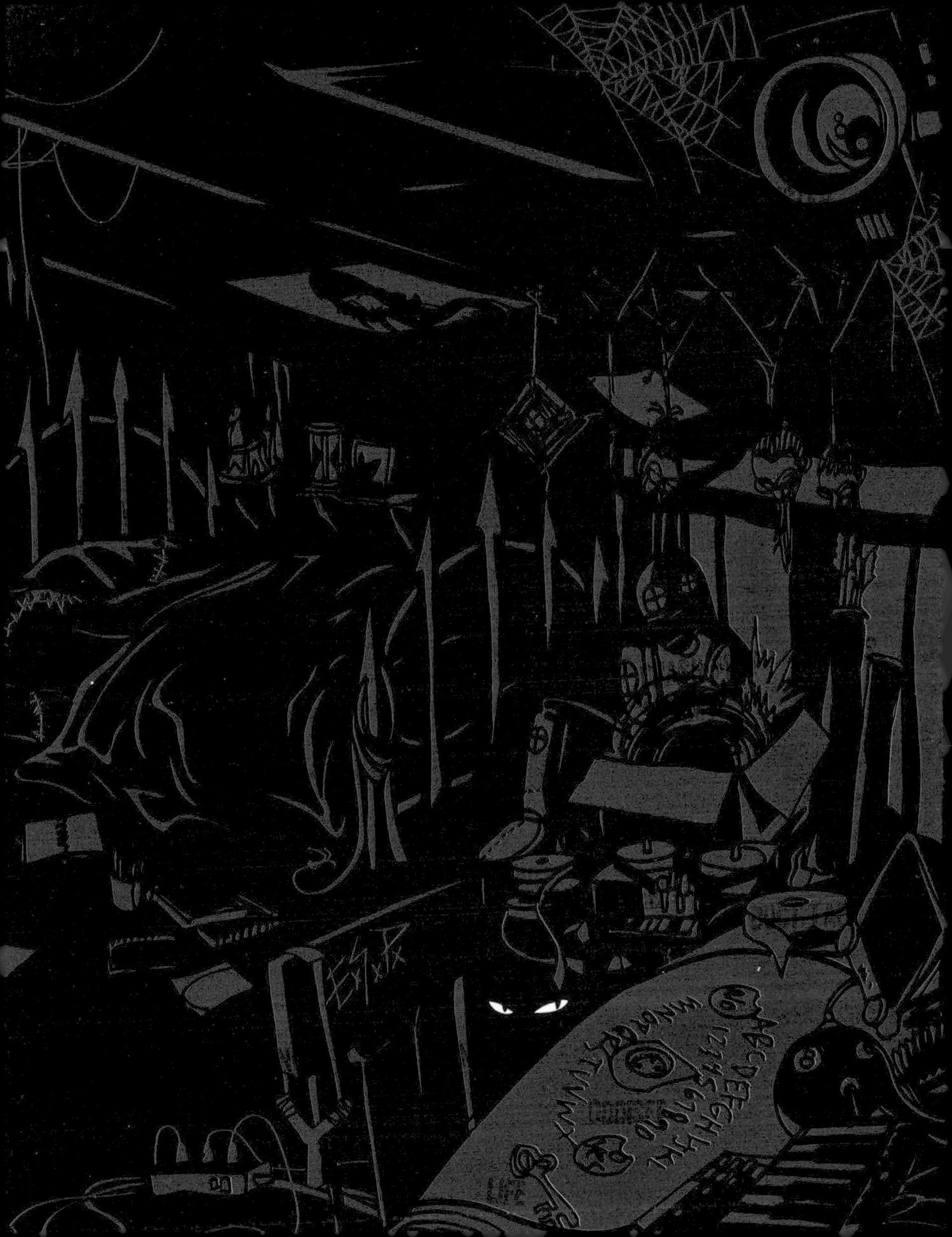

Emily sees the world
through a tangled web.

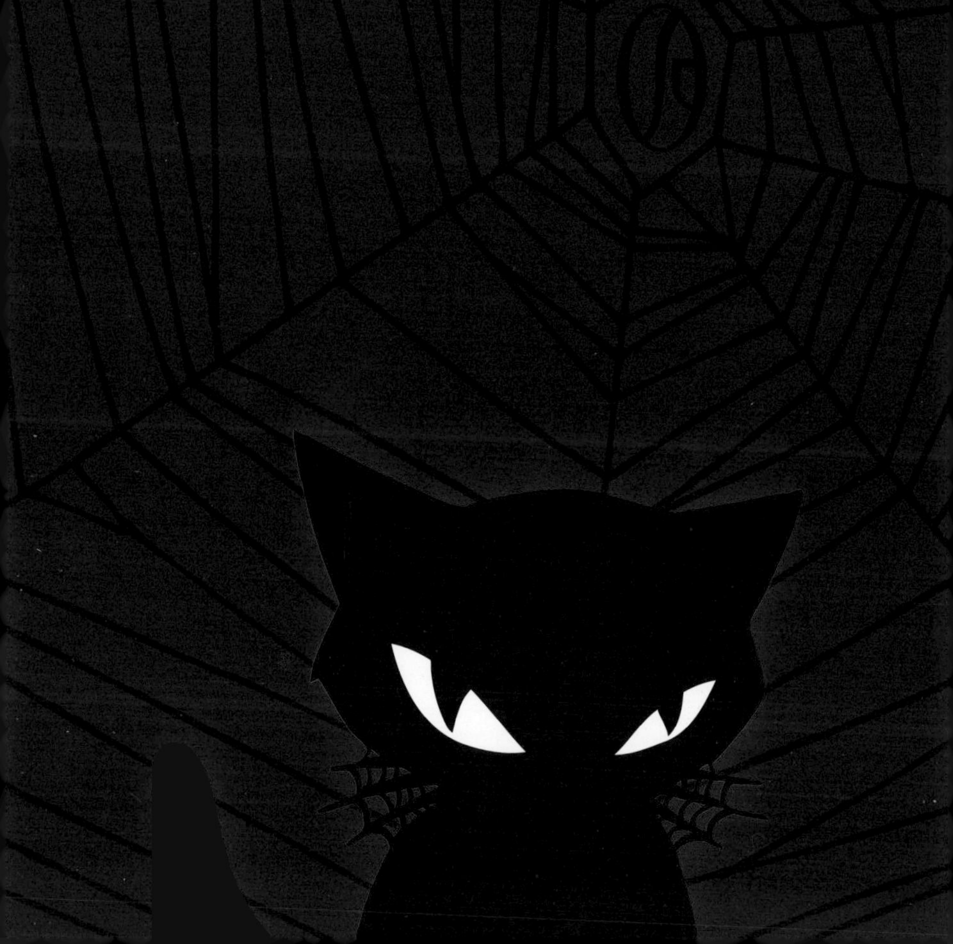

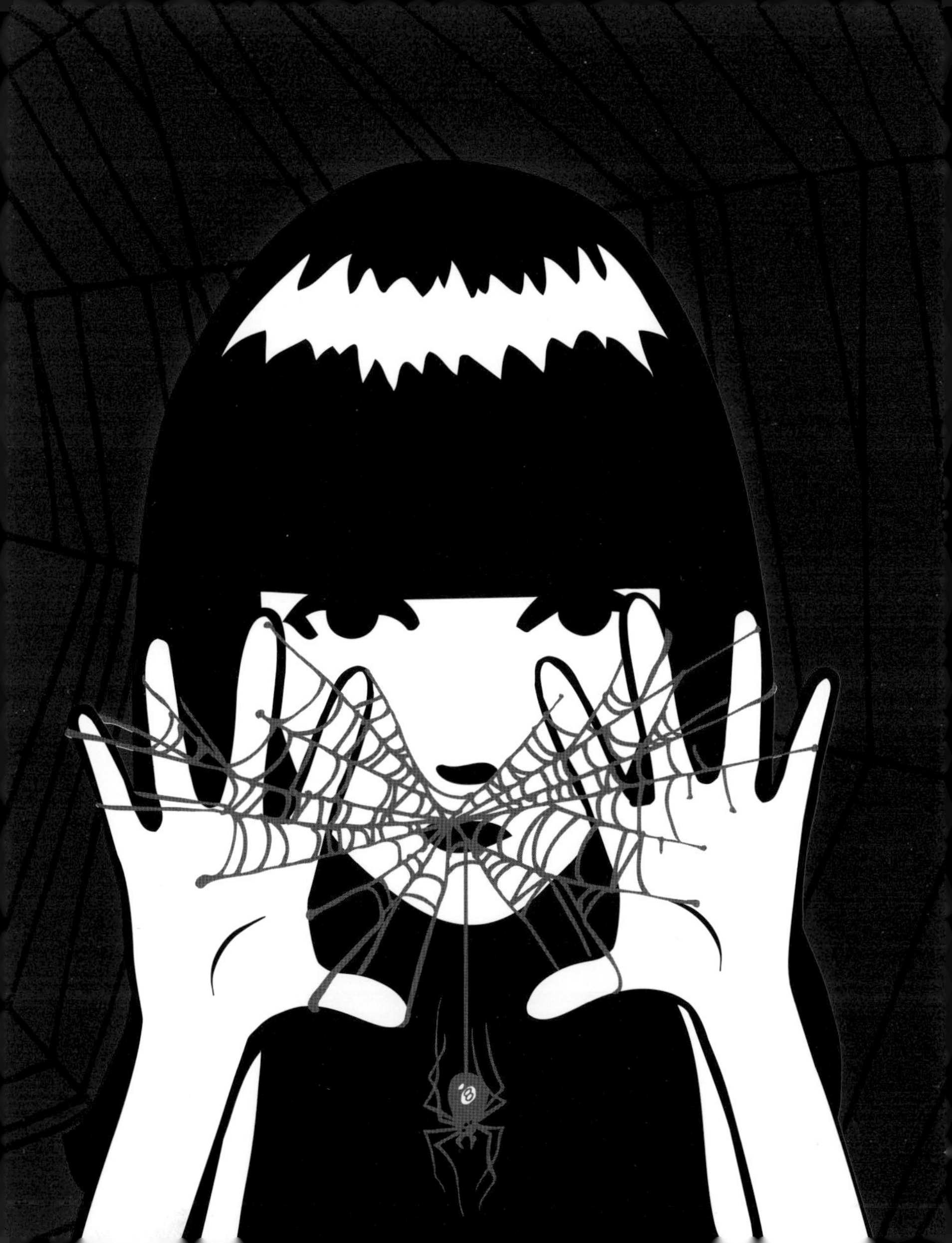

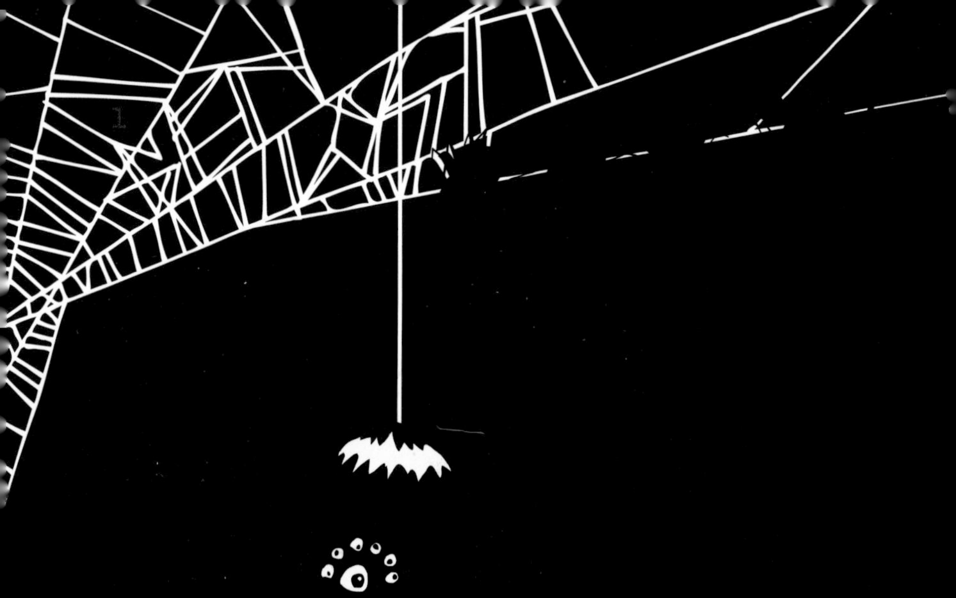

WIDE WORLD OF WEBS

	NAME	SPECIES	WEB TITLE
1)	Miss Tory	Black Widow	Message from Above
2)	Xanadu	Targon Widow	Nightshade
3)	Boris	Daddy Longlegs	Morning Star Eyes
4)	Destimona	Fat Bottom Spinner	Sabbath
5)	Poison Ivy	Furlong Widow	After Life
6)	Poison Ivy II	Furlong Widow	After After Life
7)	Cupcake	Blue Jumper	Miles
8)	Emily	Black Widow	Self Portrait
9)	Ferril	Twisted Furlong	Posse
10)	Dr. Know	Hopping Pitster	Abstract Ozzy
11)	Bloody Mary	Brazilian Webster	Revolution
12)	Charlotte	Queen Diamond	God's Eye
13)	Sophia	Household Spider	The Amelia Rose

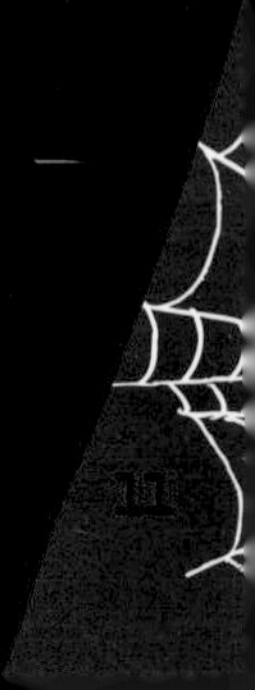

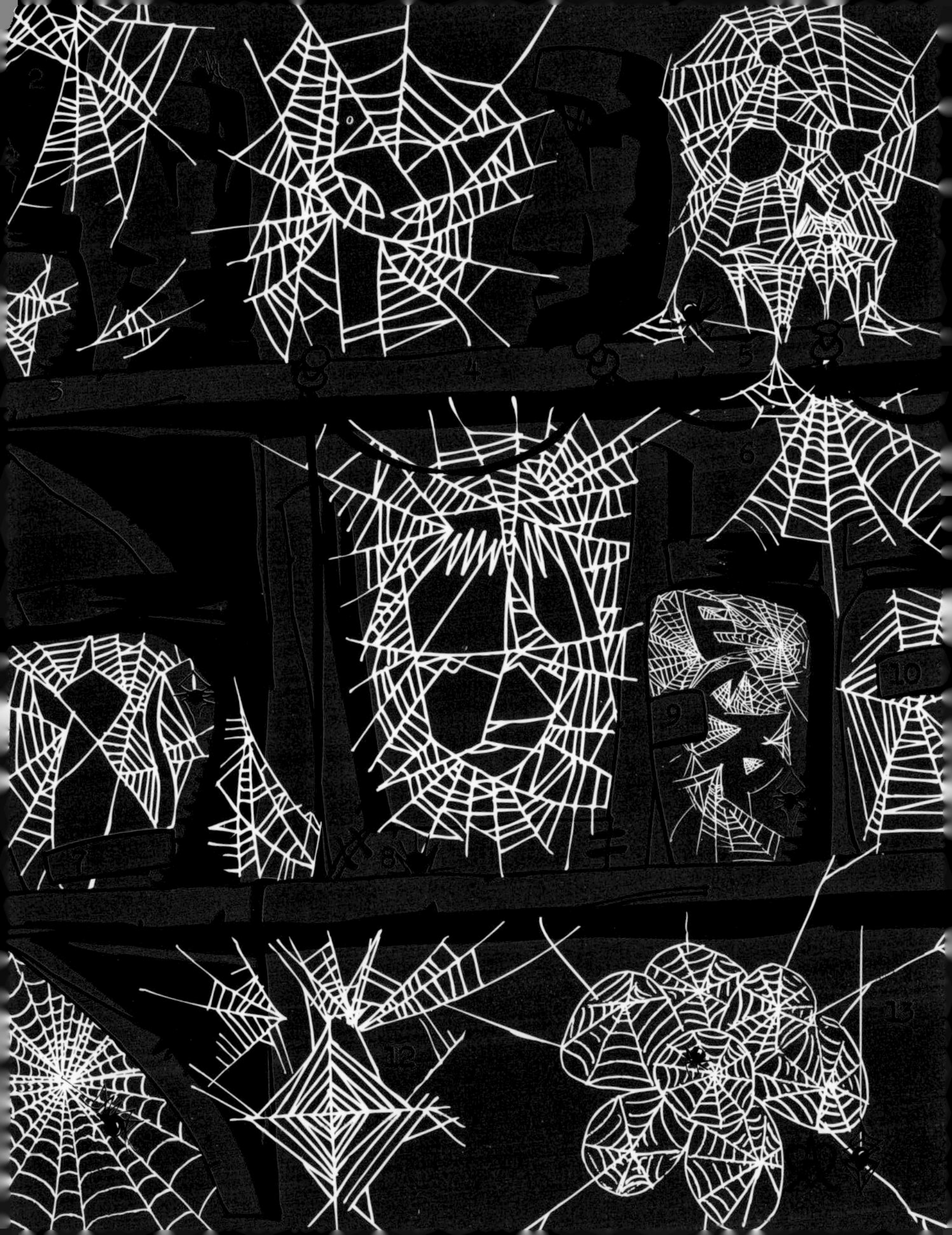
4
5
6
9
10
12
13

HEAR
STRANGE

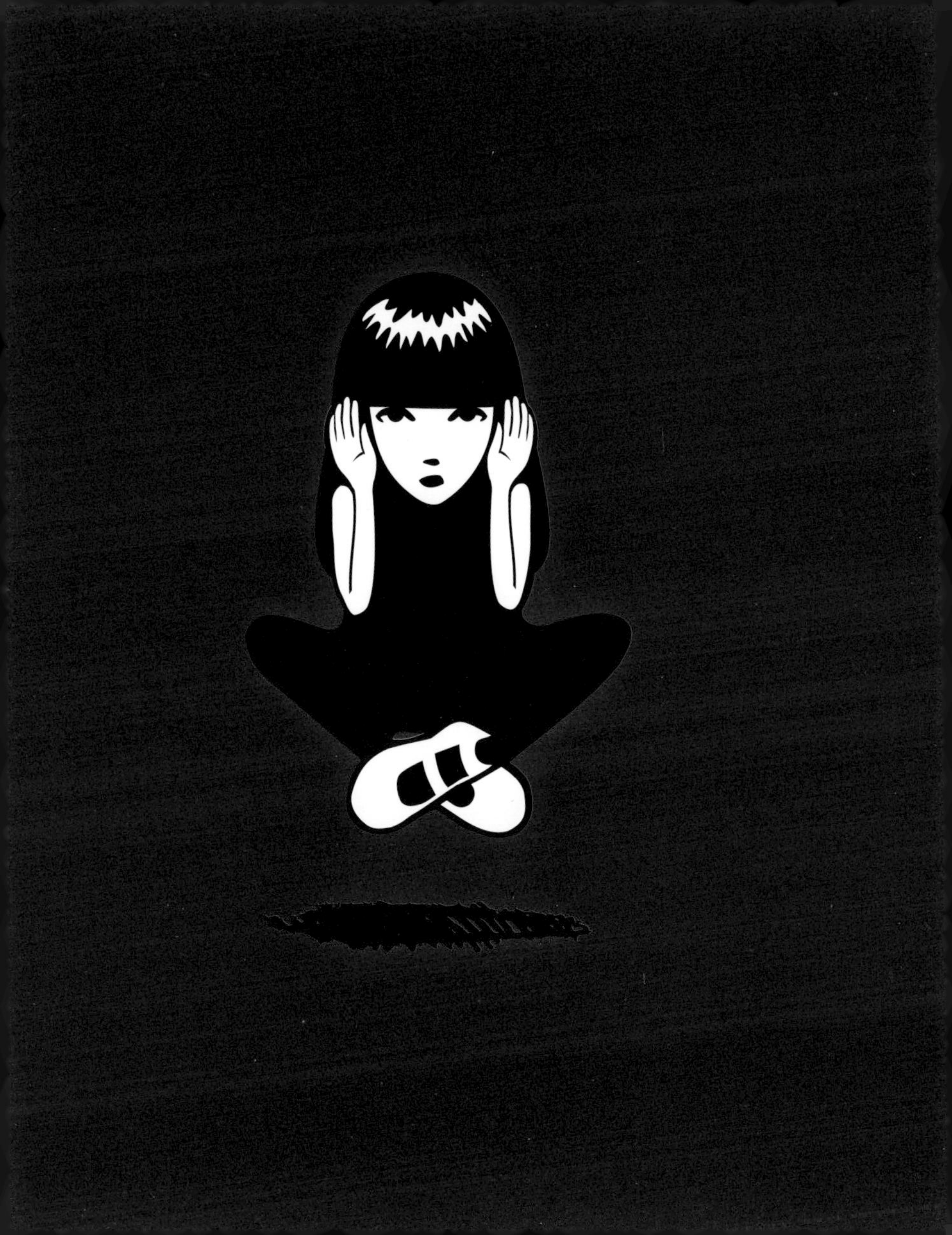

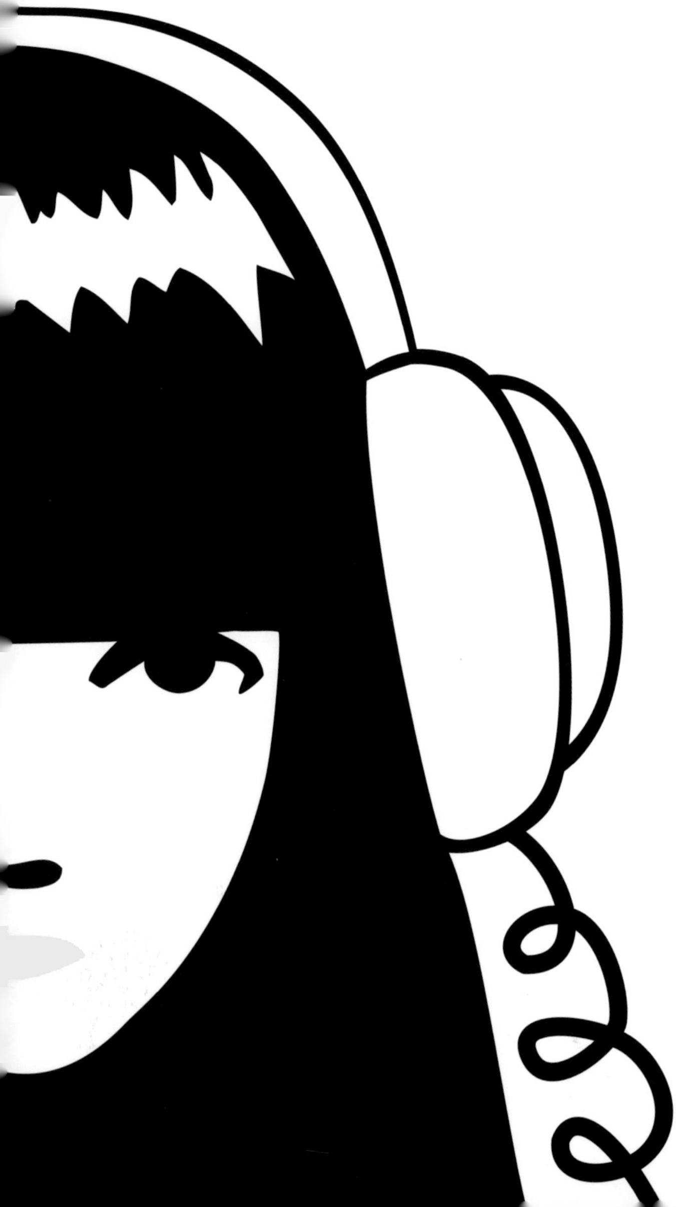

Emily hears everything...

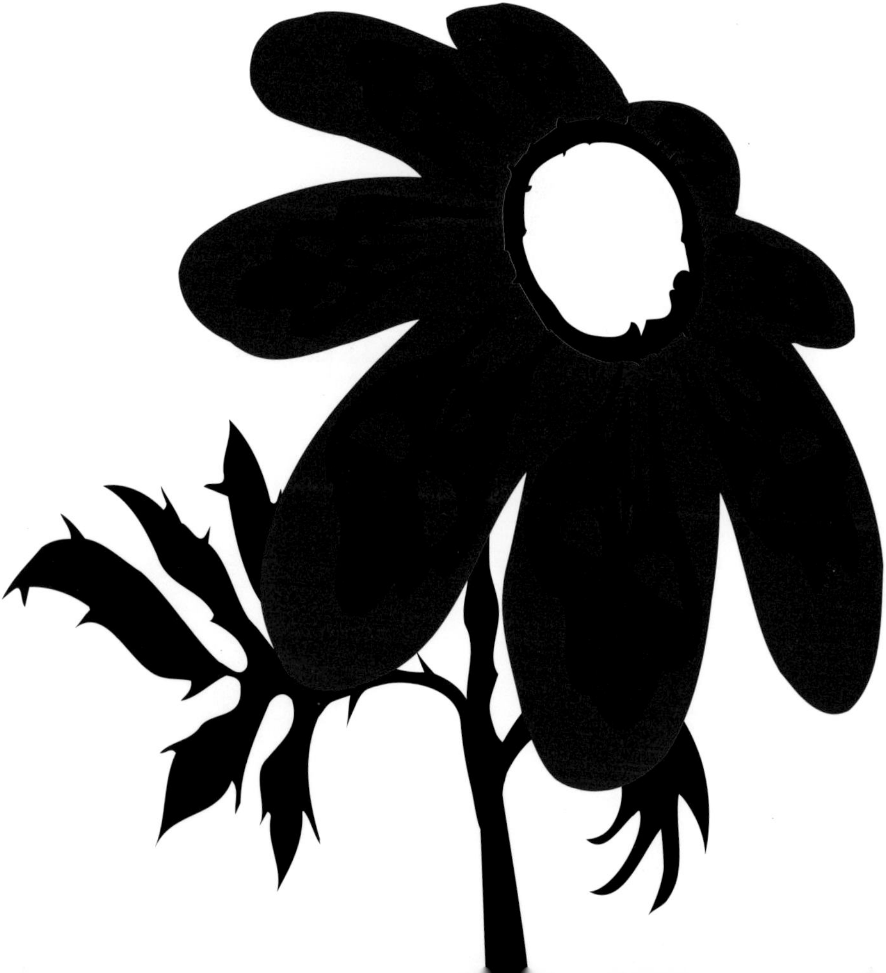

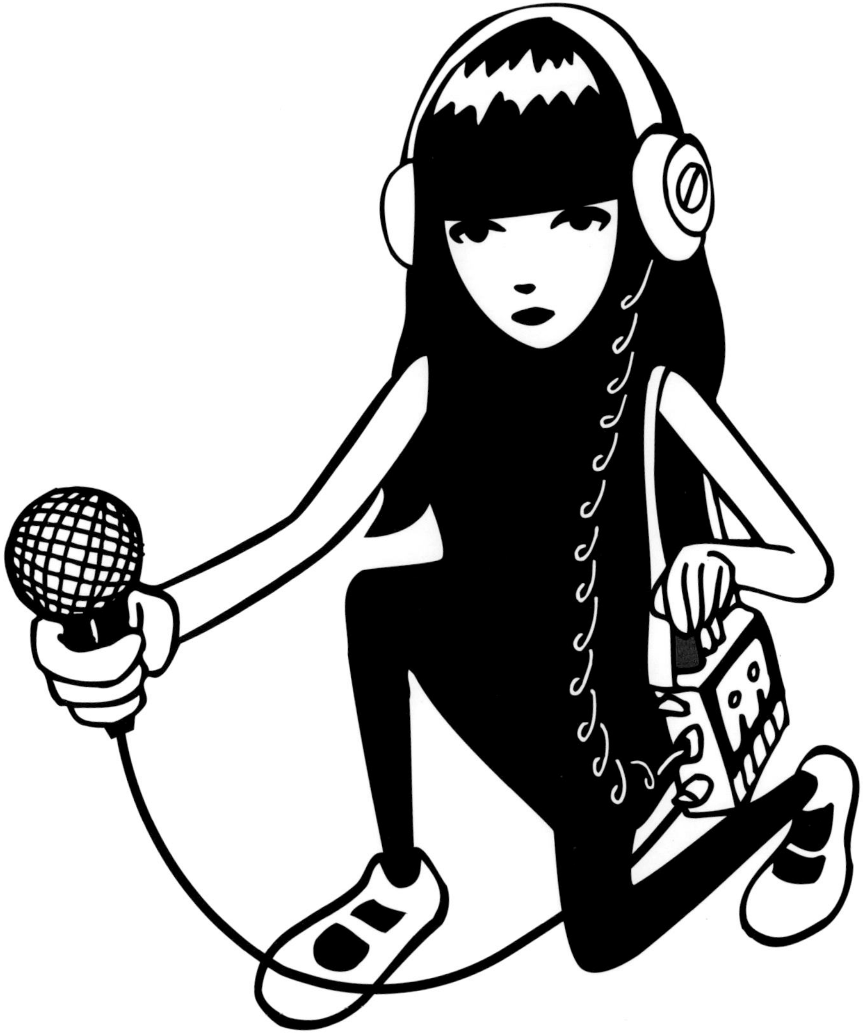

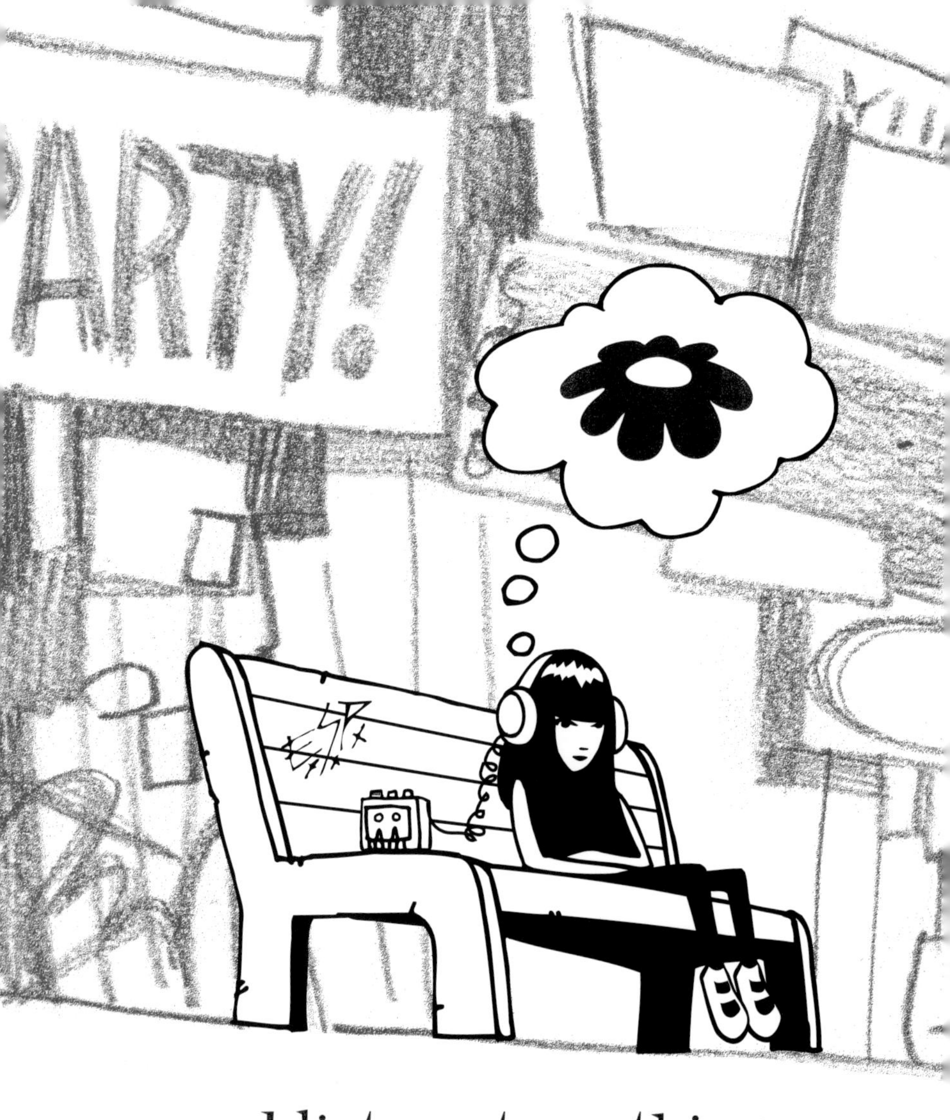
ARTY!

...and listens to nothing.

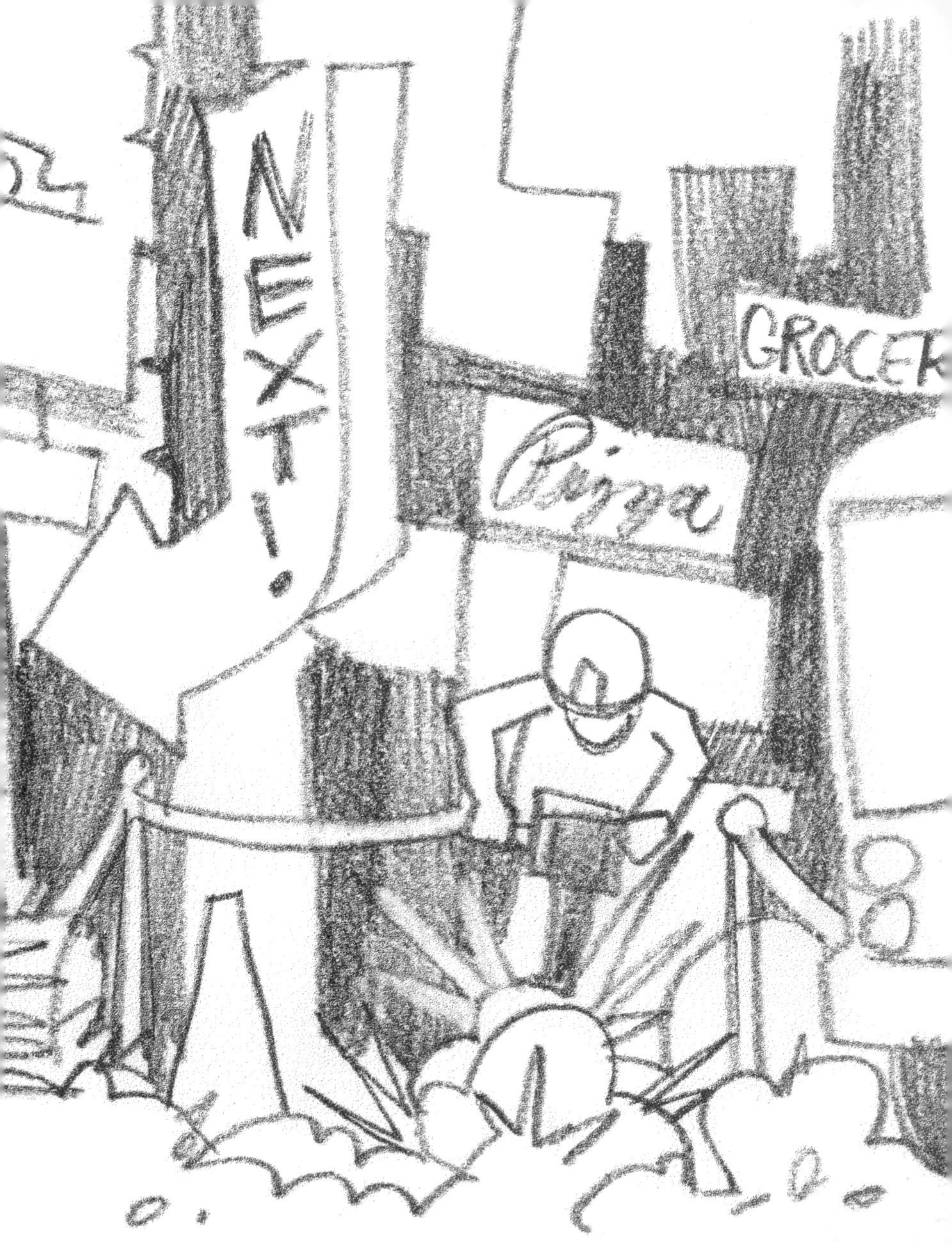
NEXT!
Pizza
GROCER

SPEAK

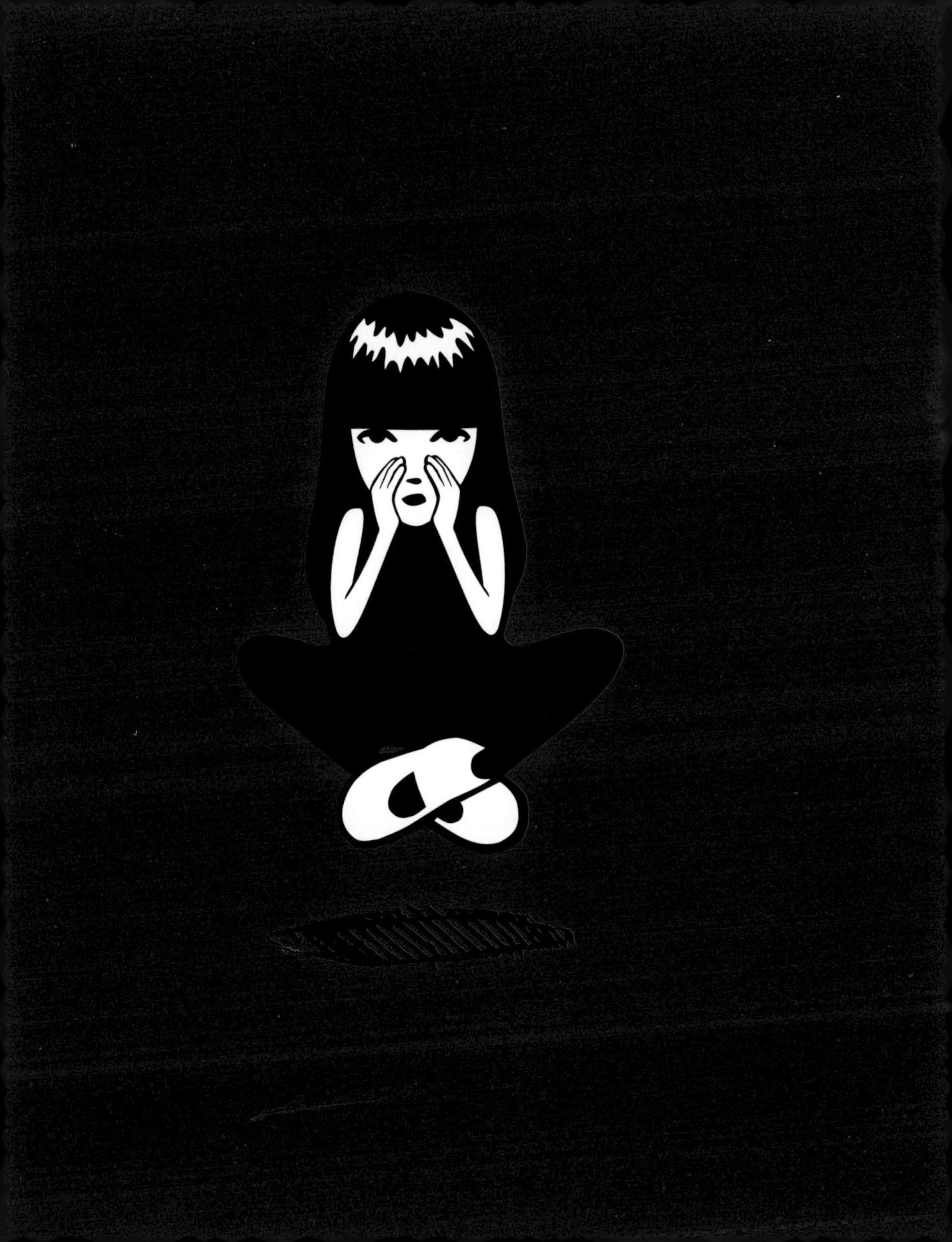

Emily may speak softly...

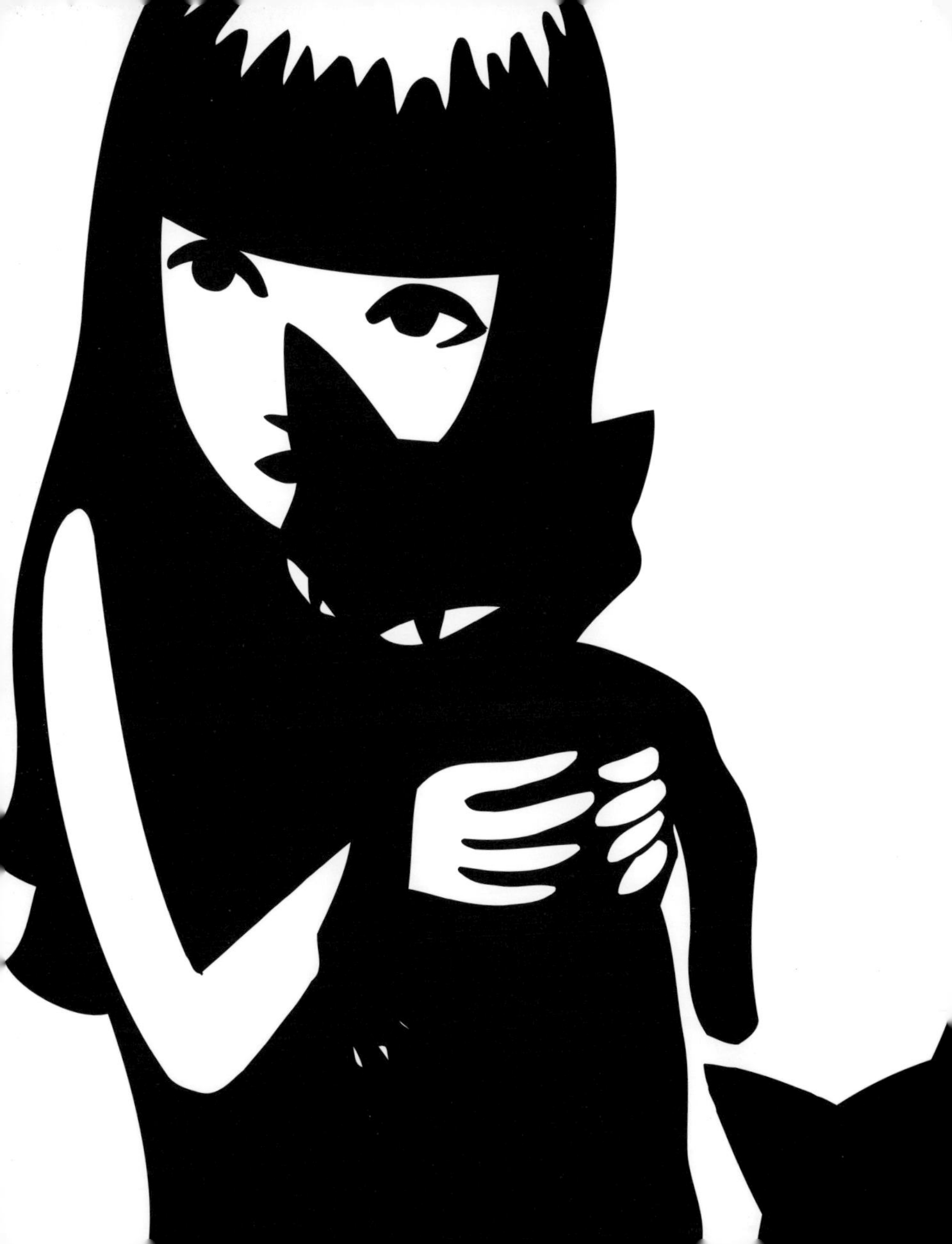

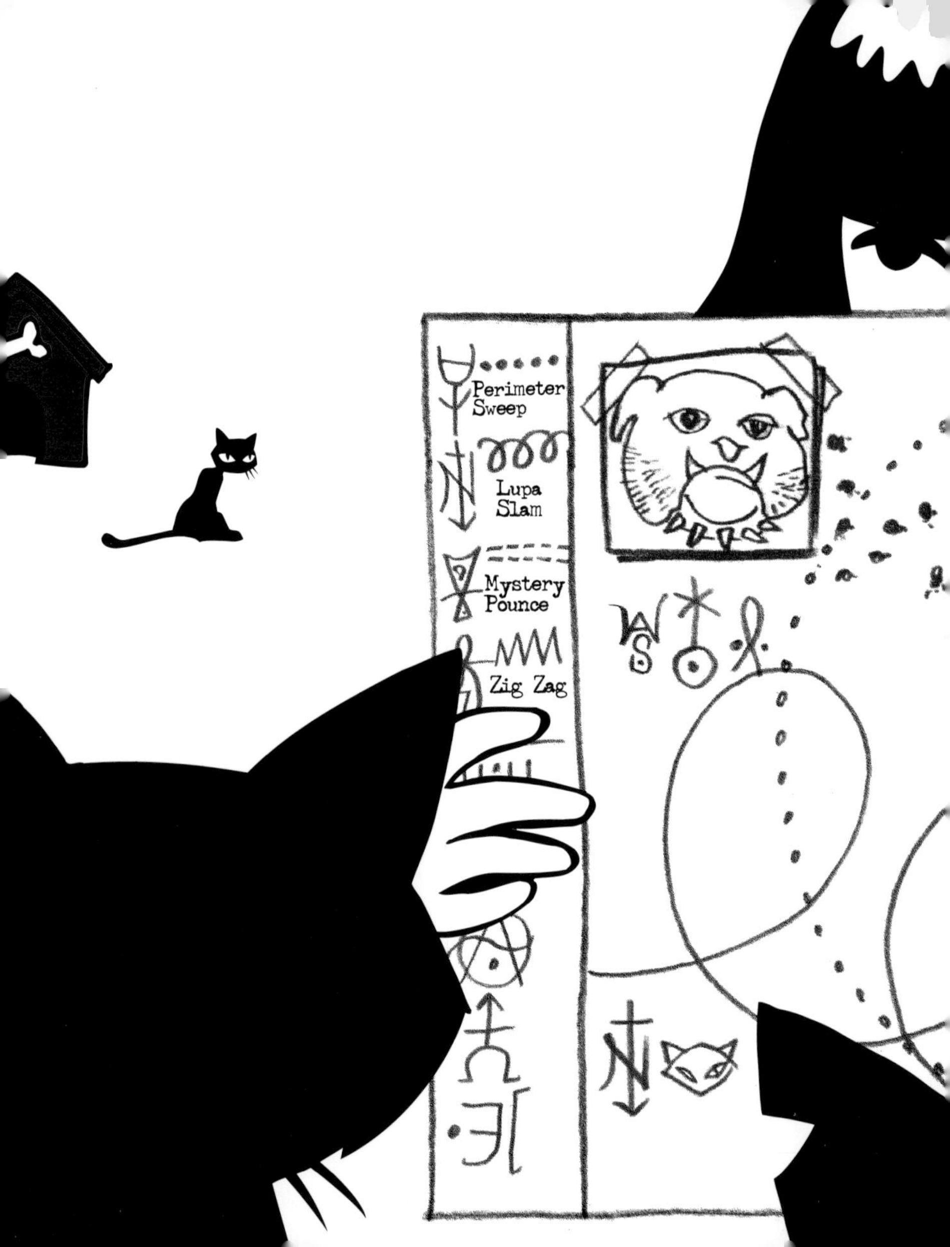

Perimeter Sweep
Lupa Slam
Mystery Pounce
Zig Zag

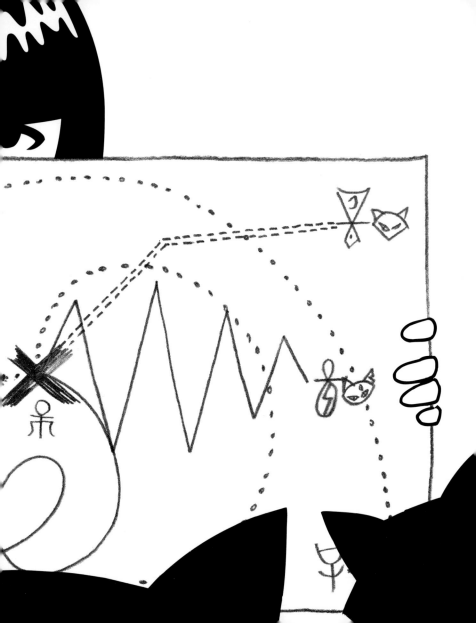

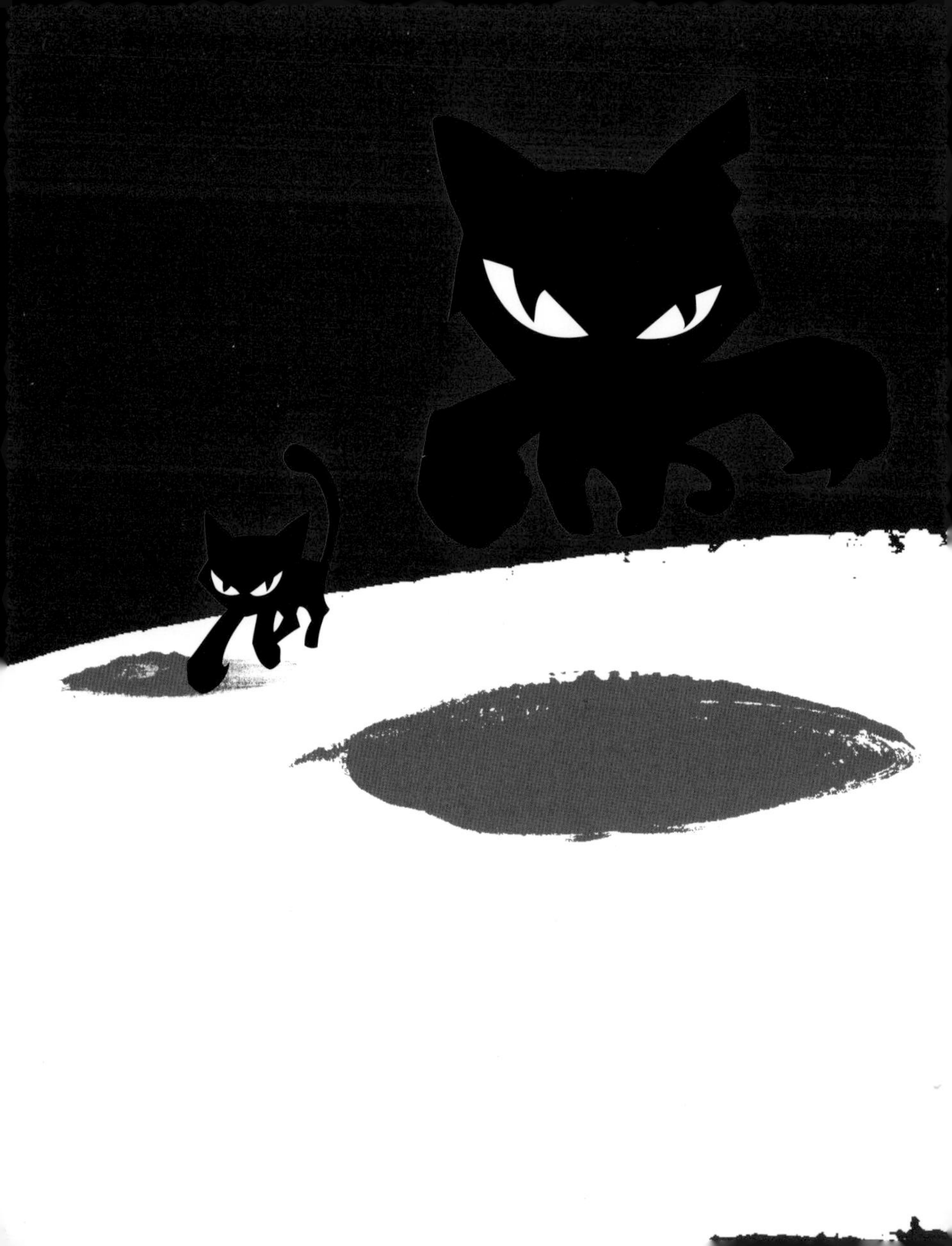

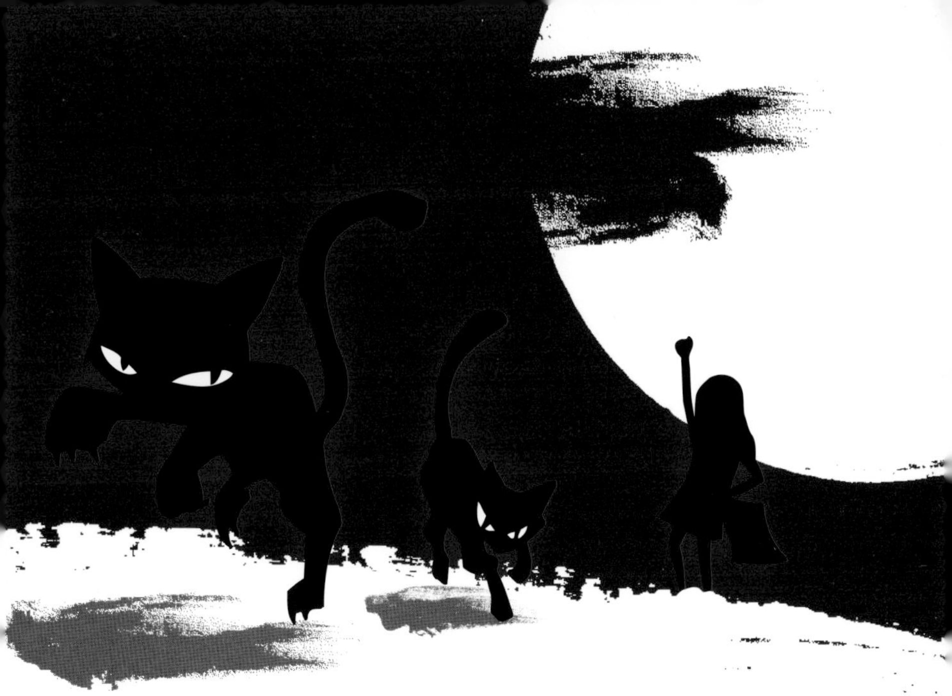

...but she is always
loud and clear.

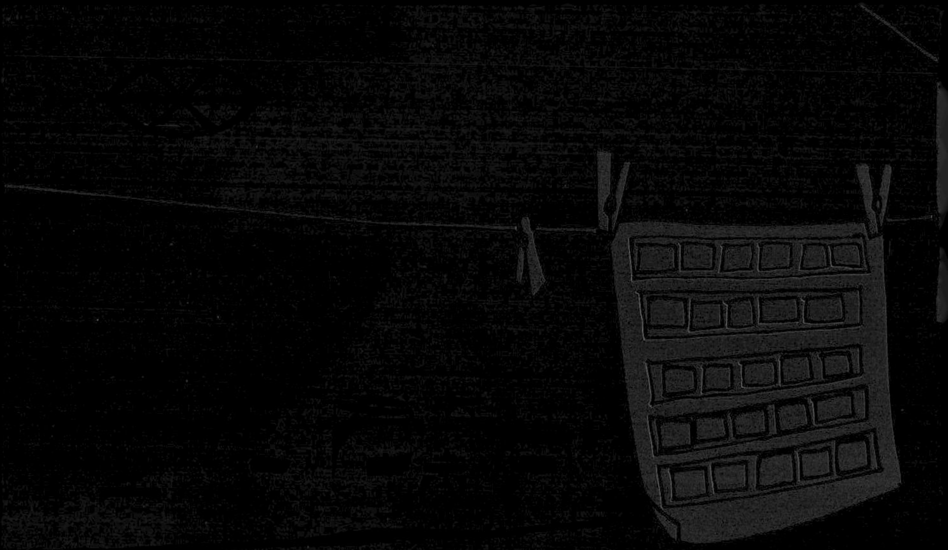

A picture speaks
a thousand weirds.

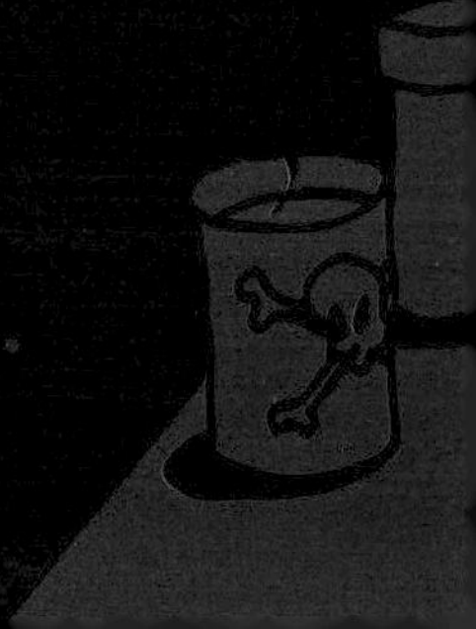

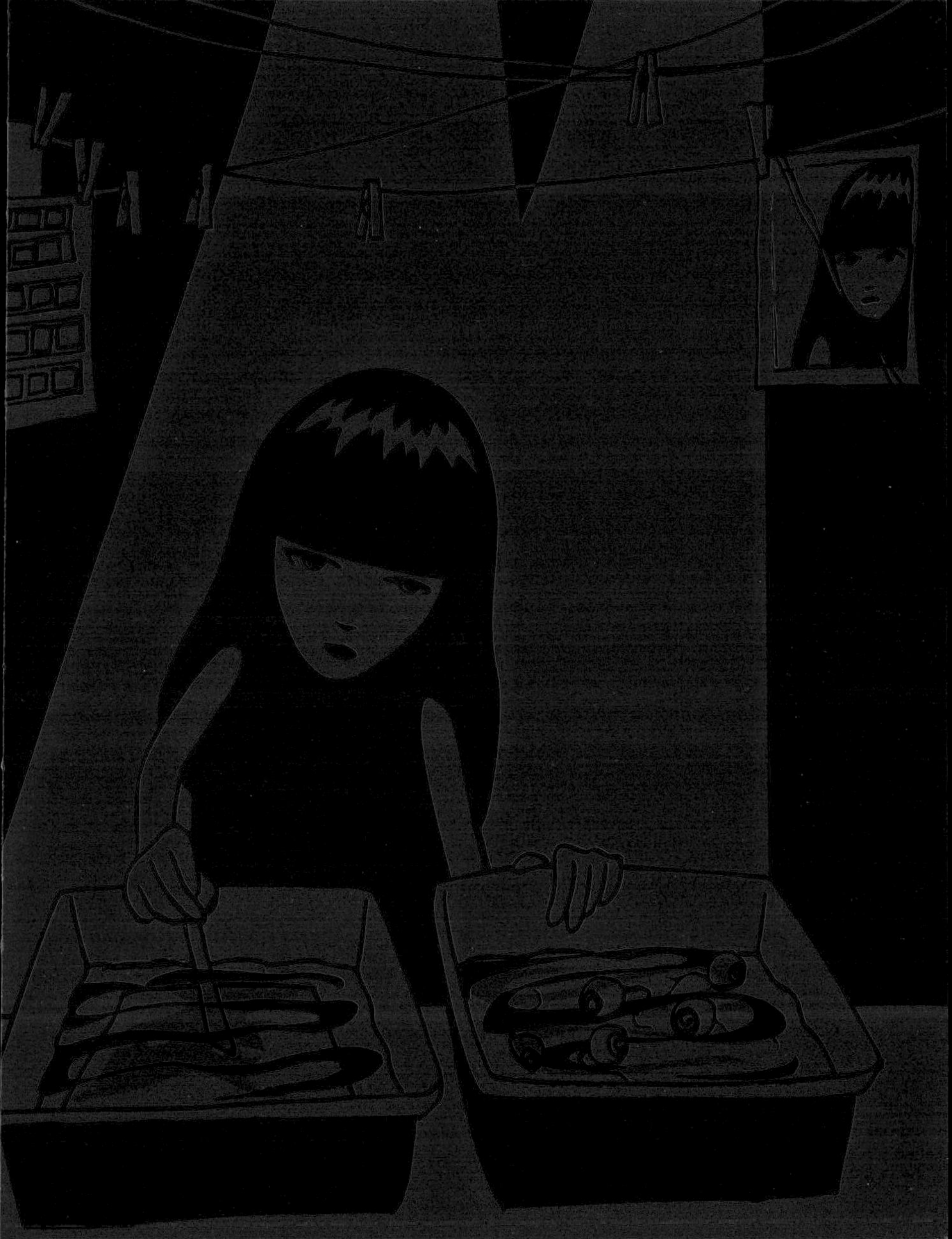

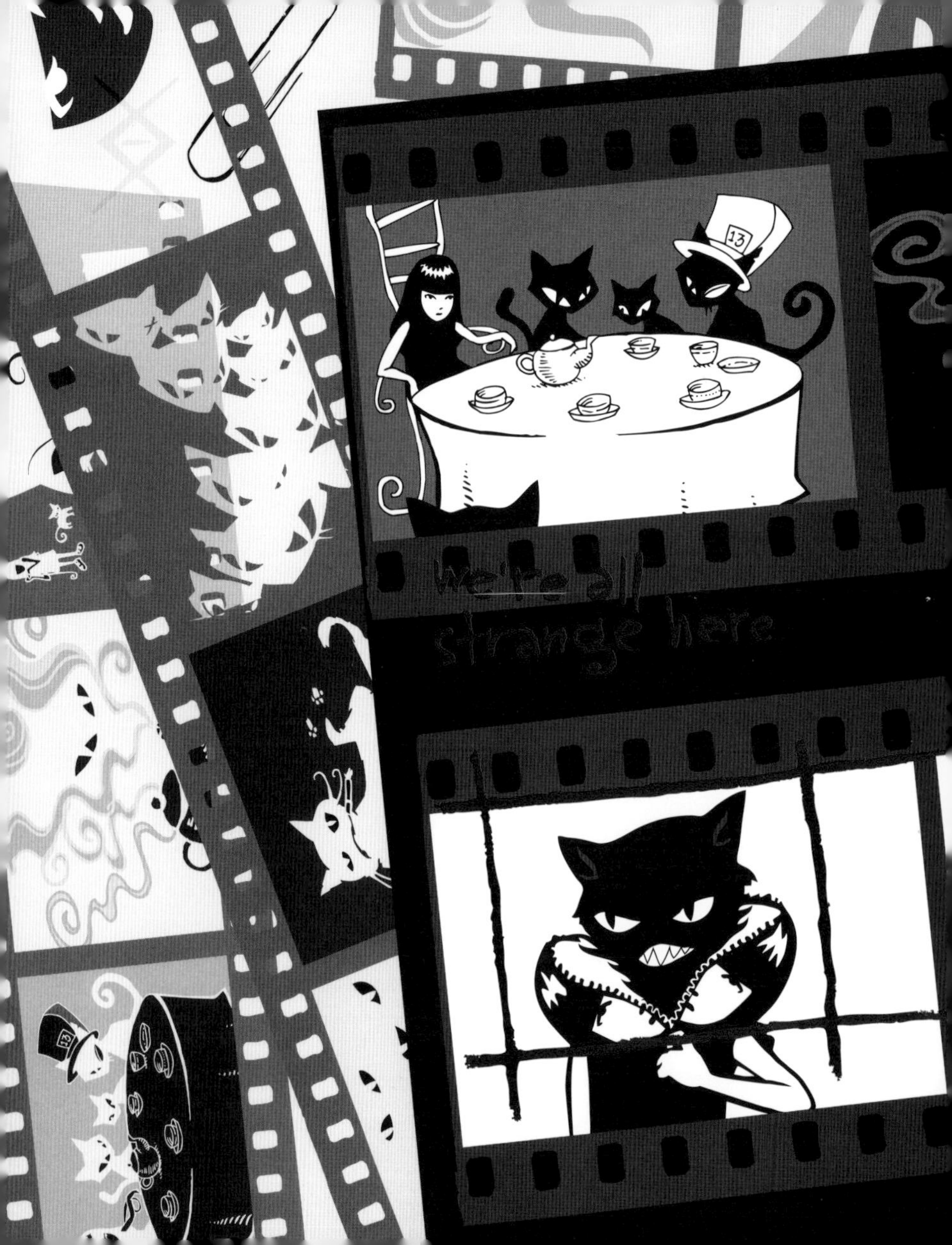
We're all
strange here

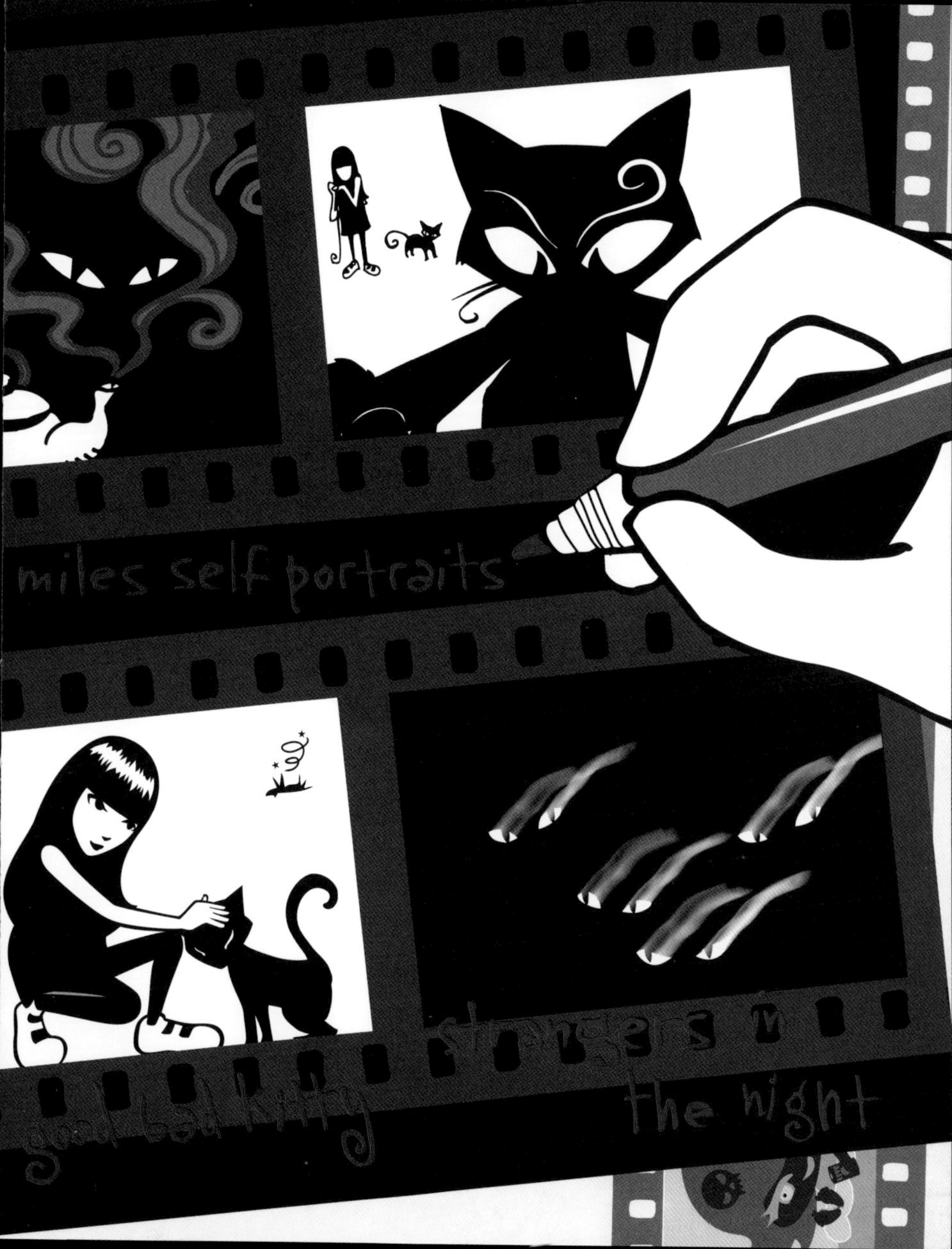

miles self portraits
good bad kitty
strangers in the night

THINK
STRANGE

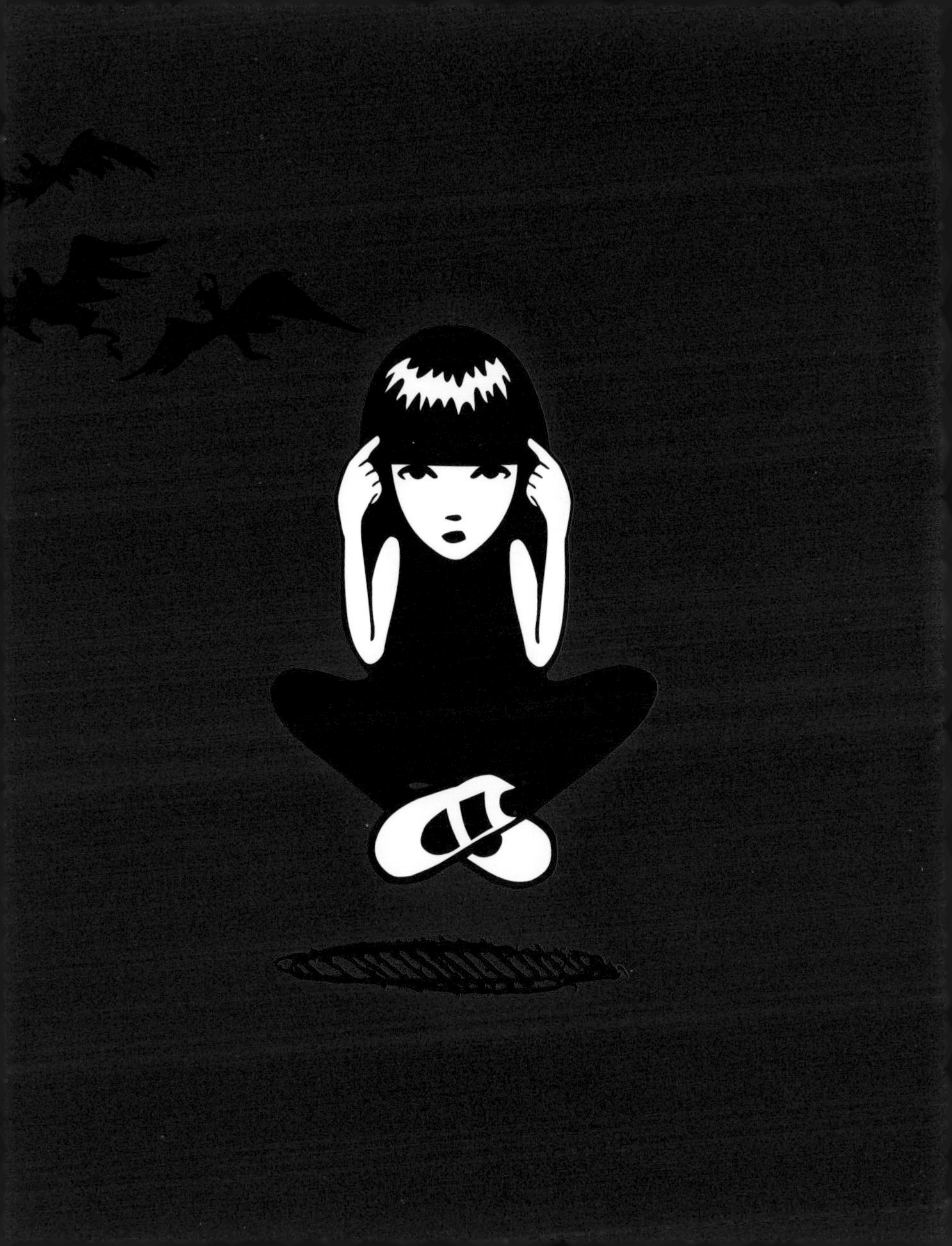

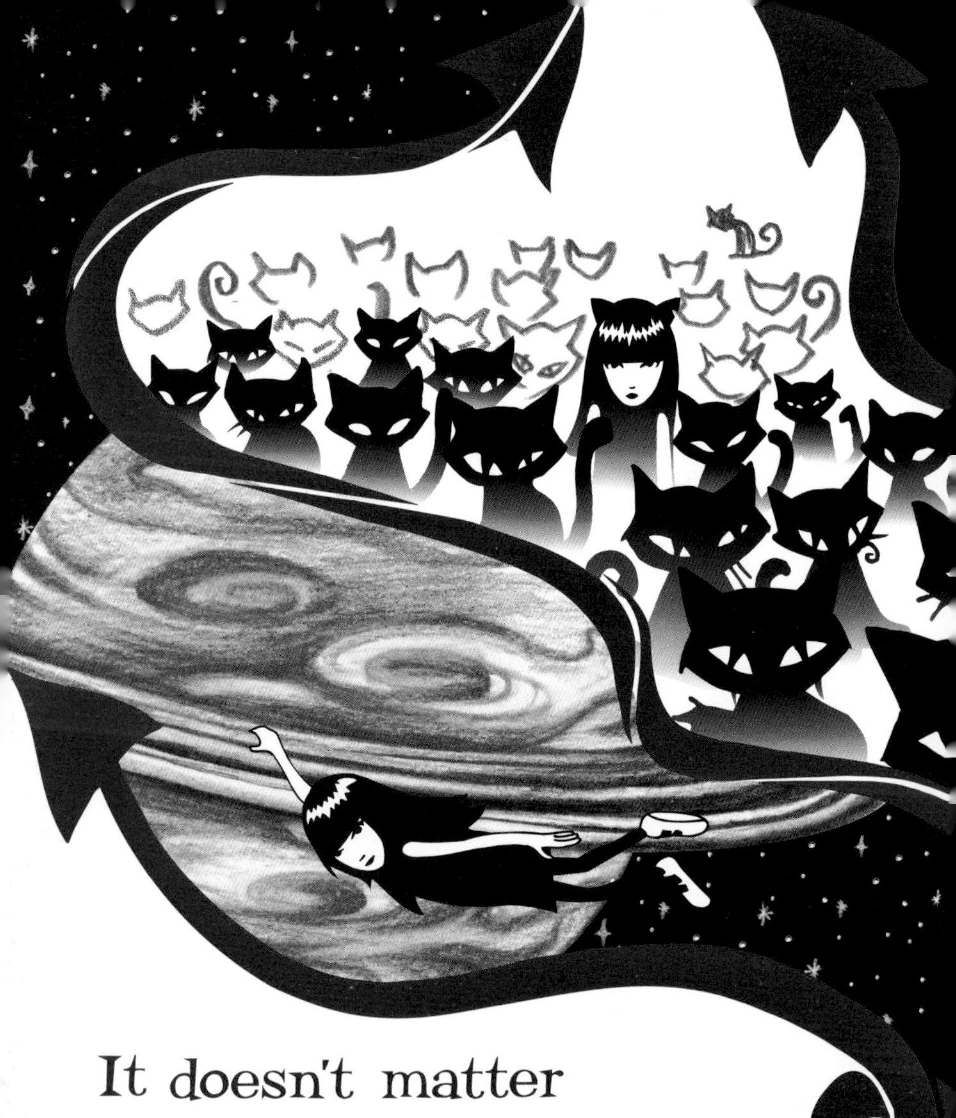

It doesn't matter
which way you go...

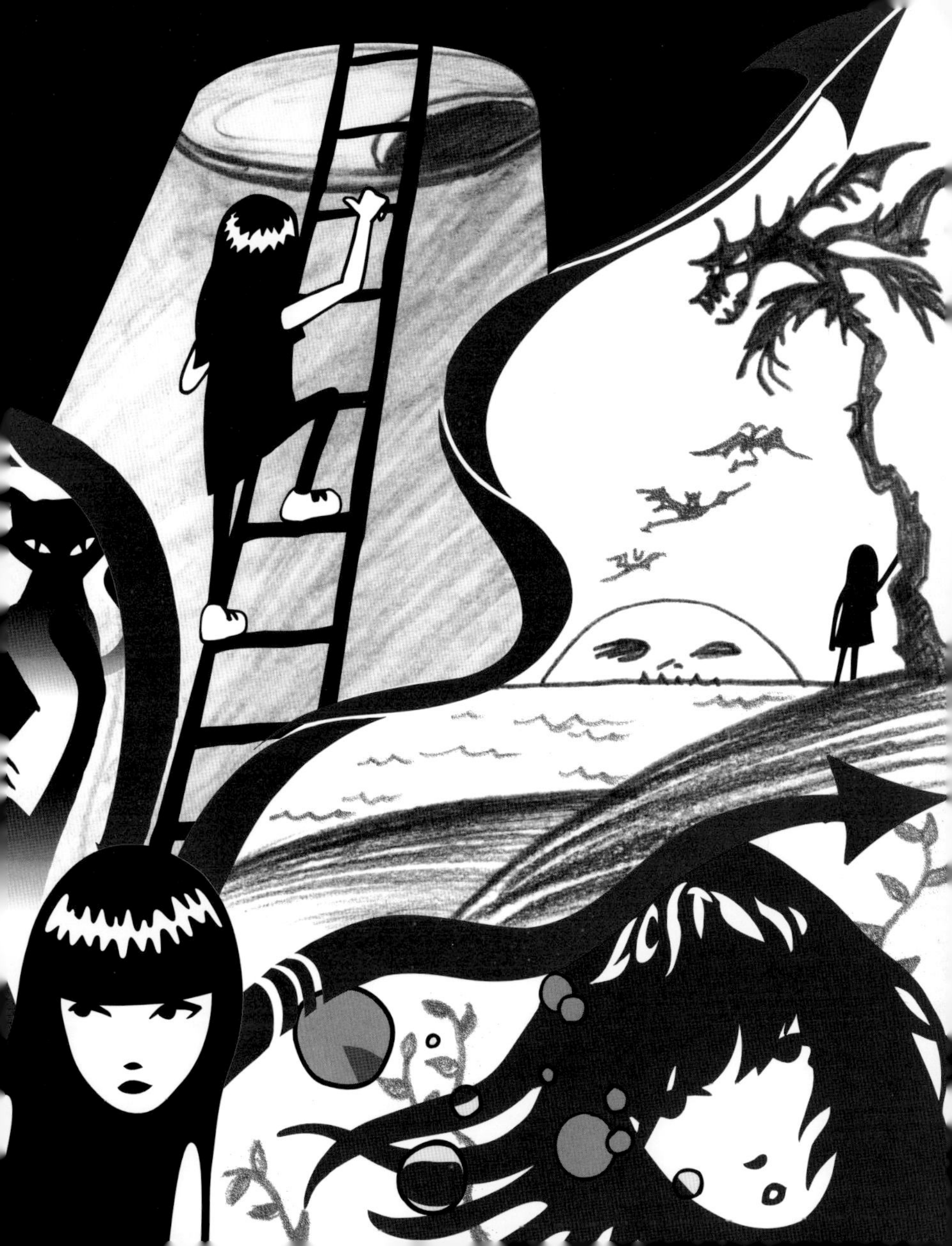

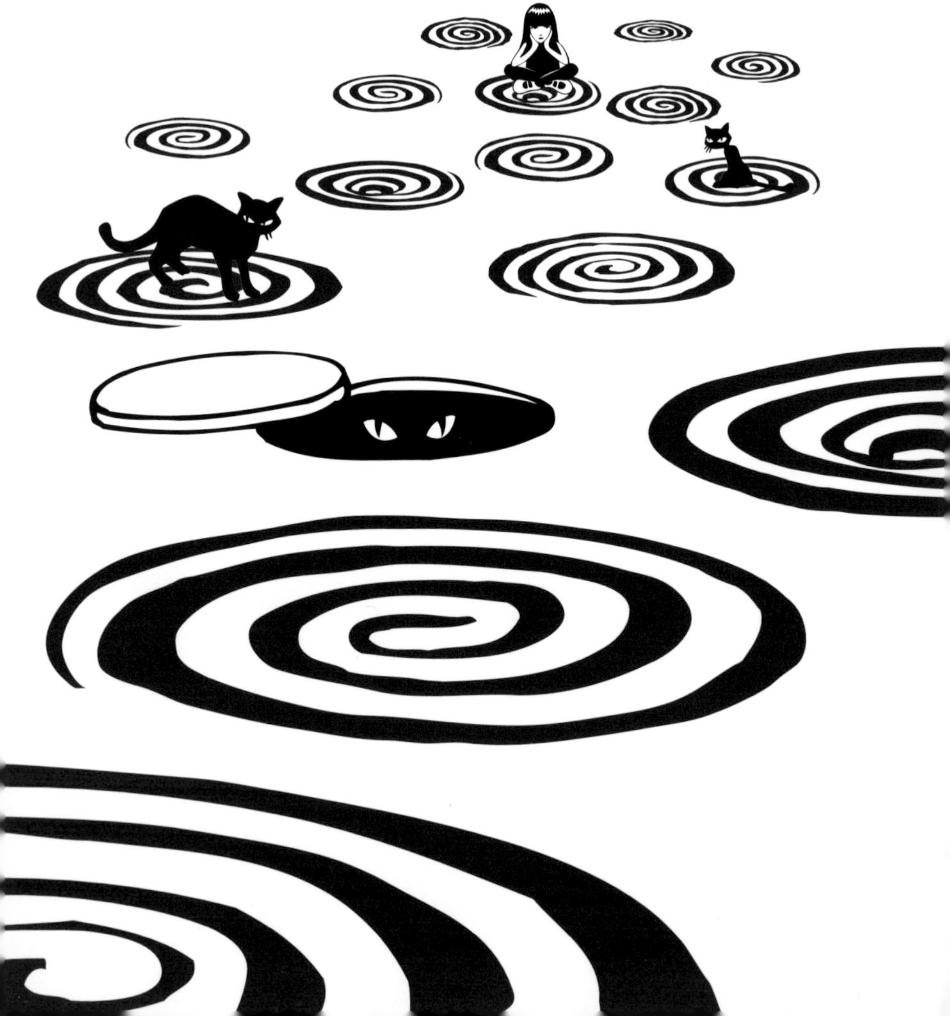

...as long as you
get lost.

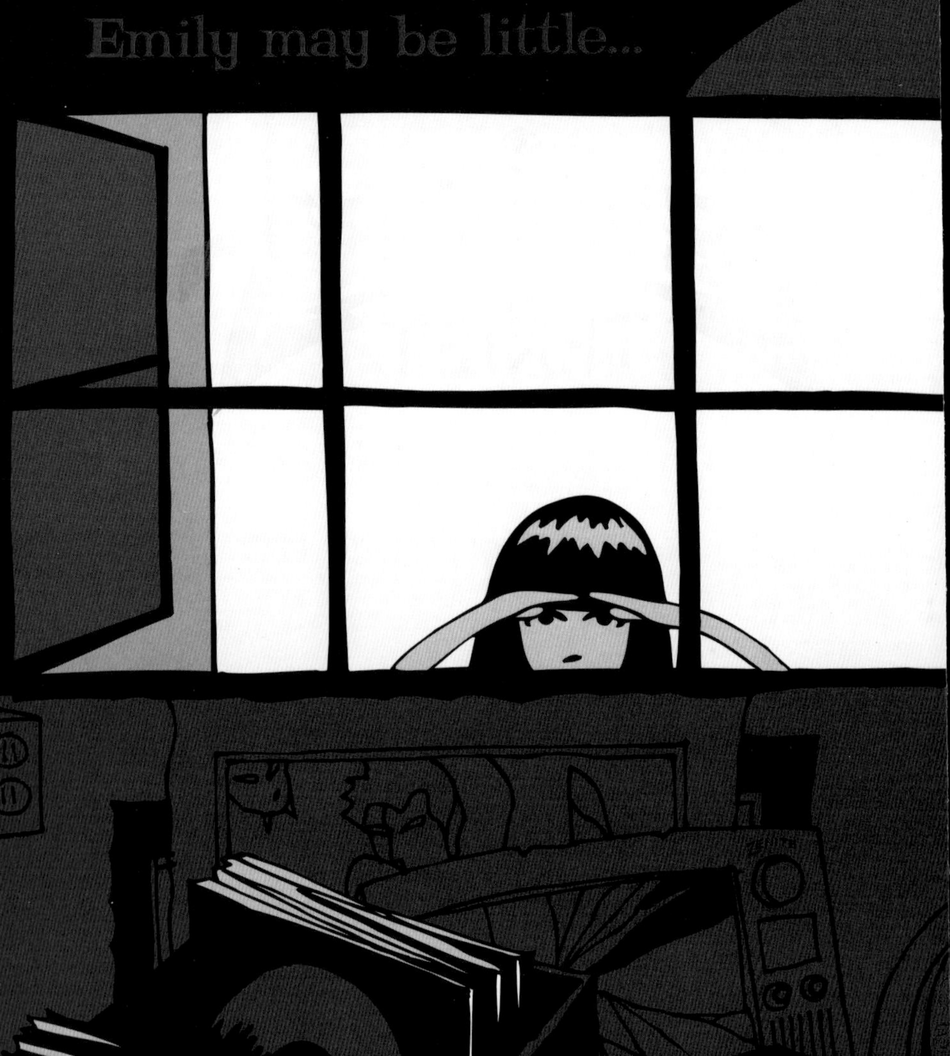
Emily may be little...

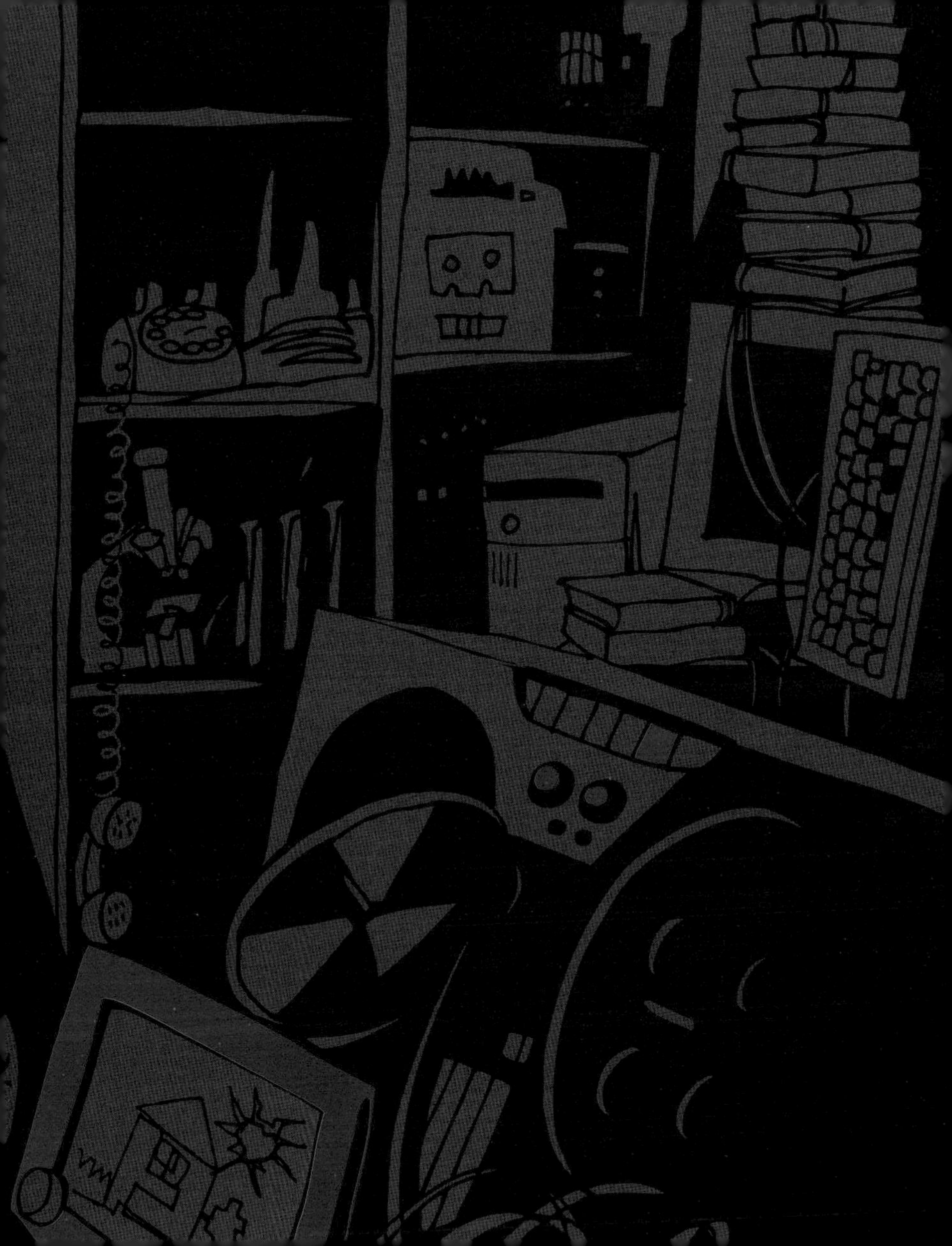

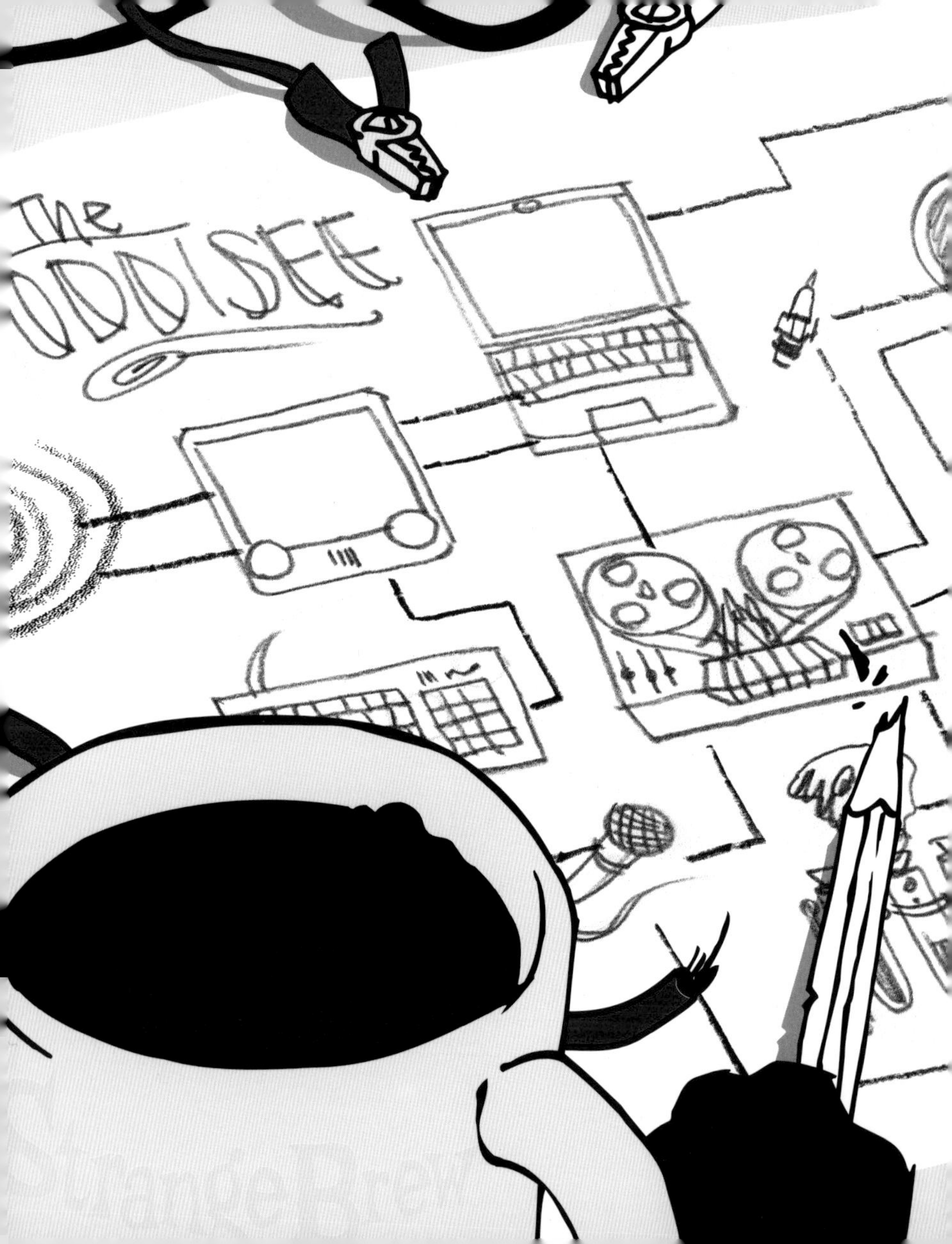

The
ODDISEE

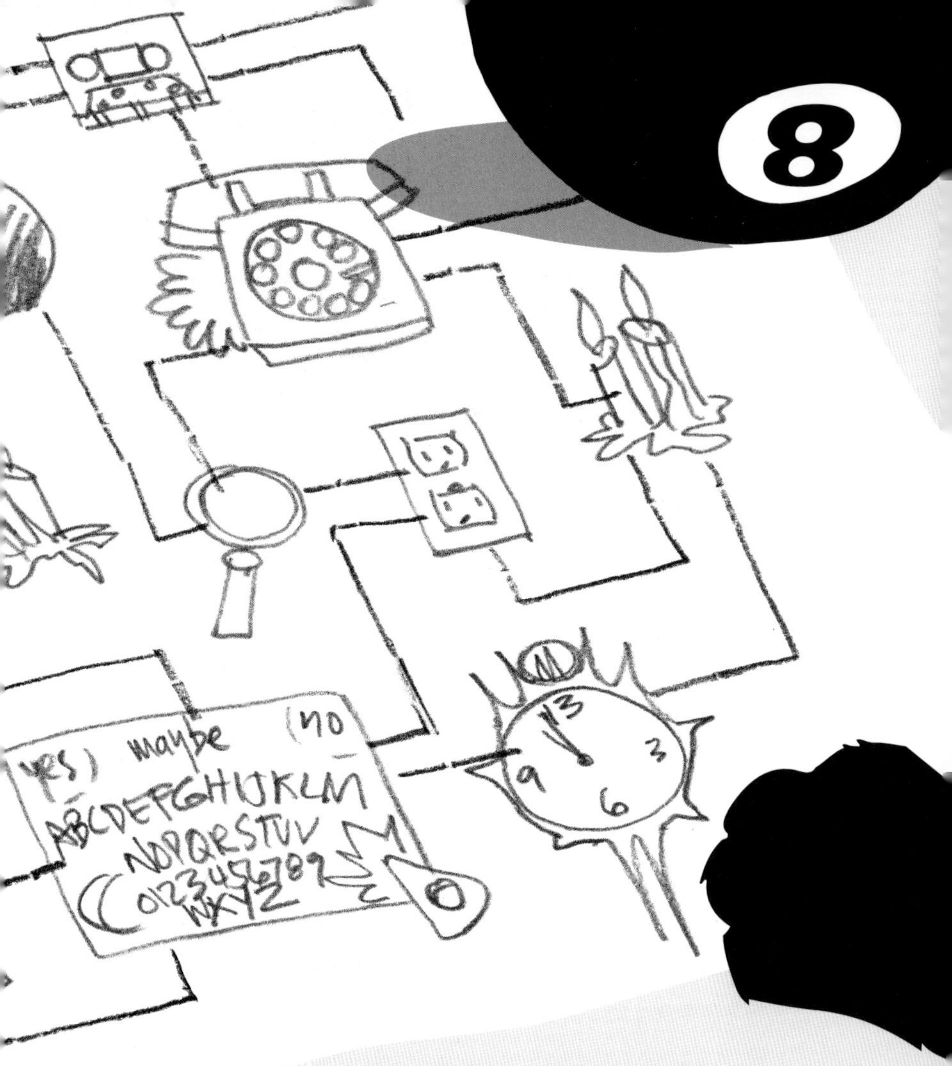
8
YES
maybe
NO

...but she thinks big.

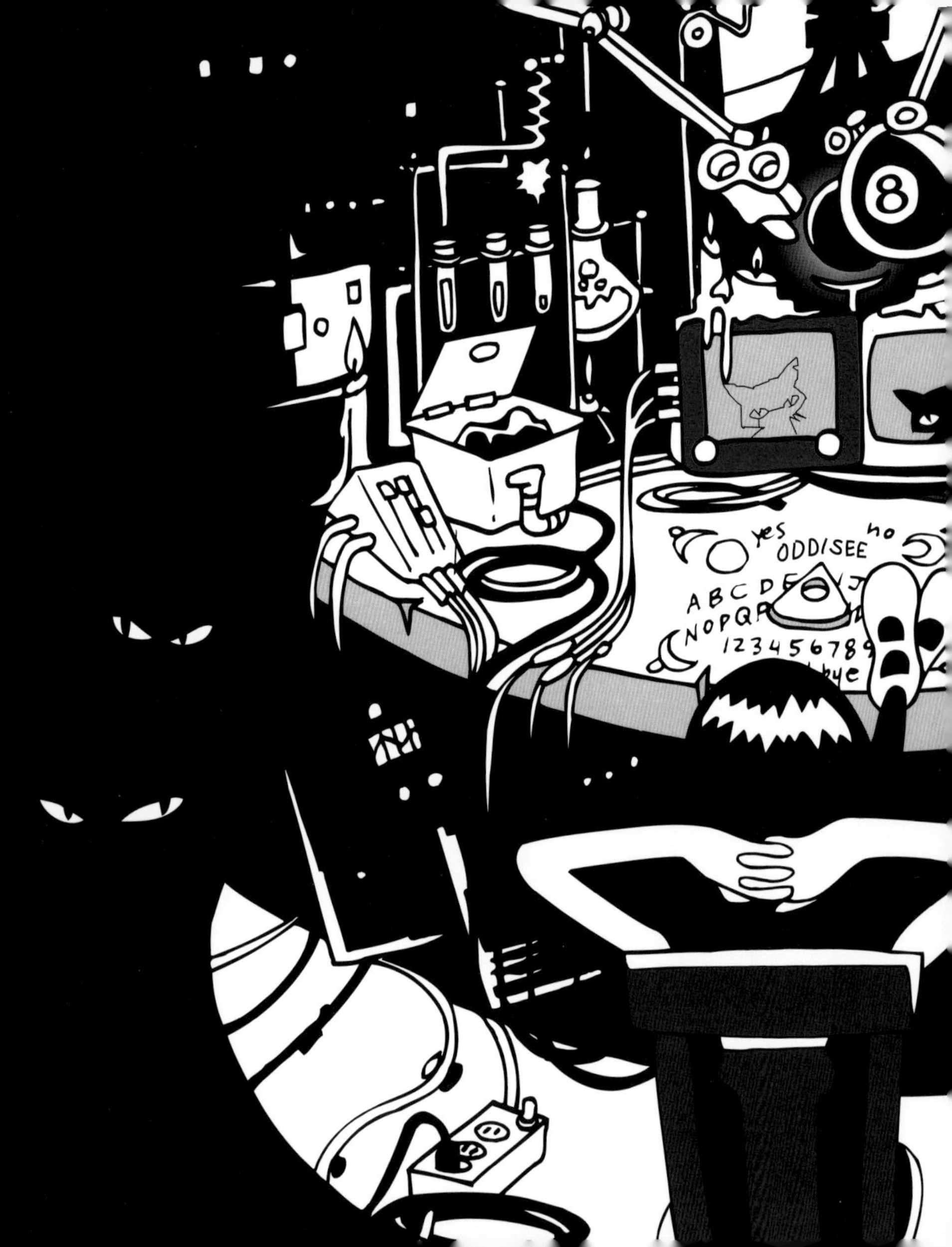
yes
no
ODDISEE

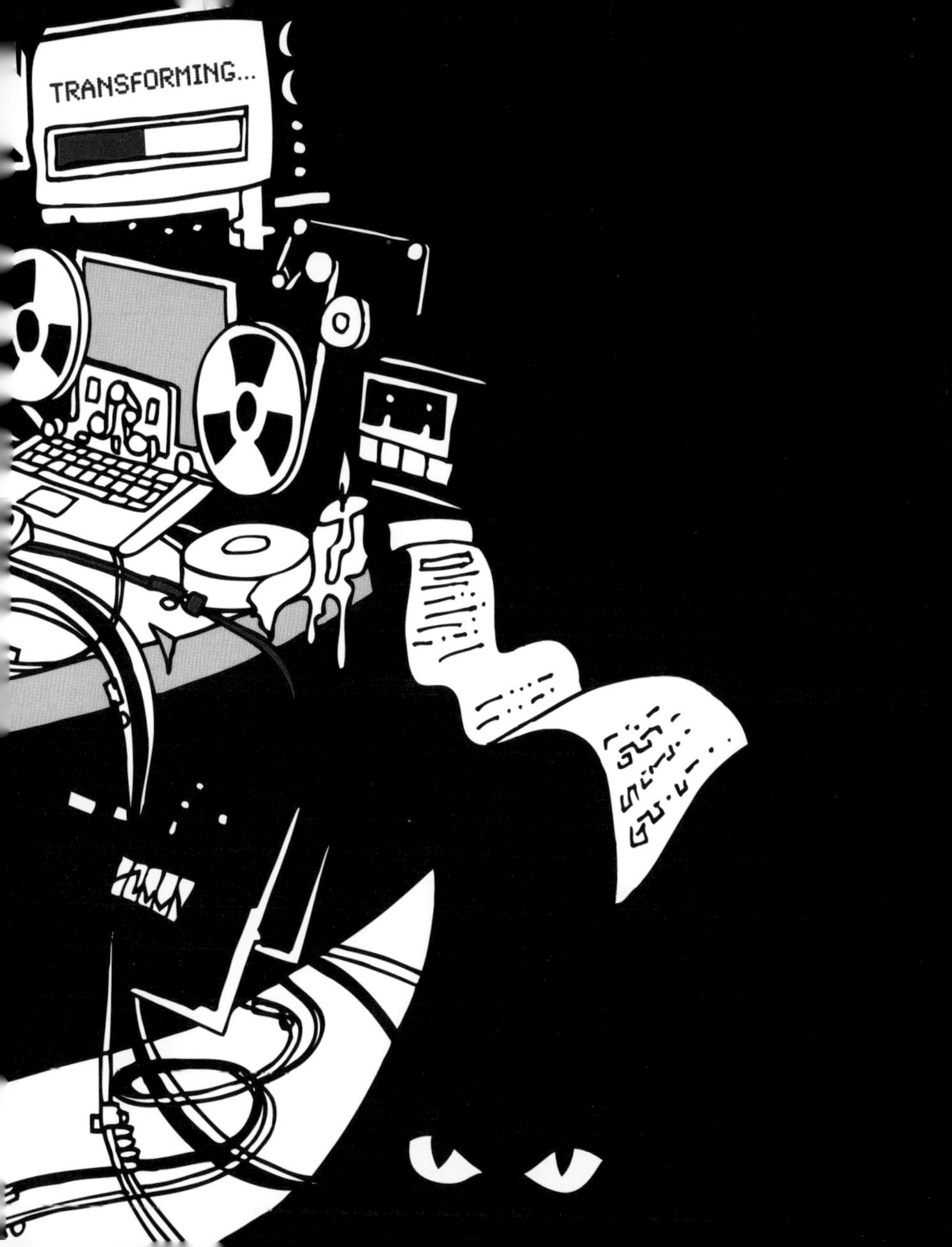
TRANSFORMING...

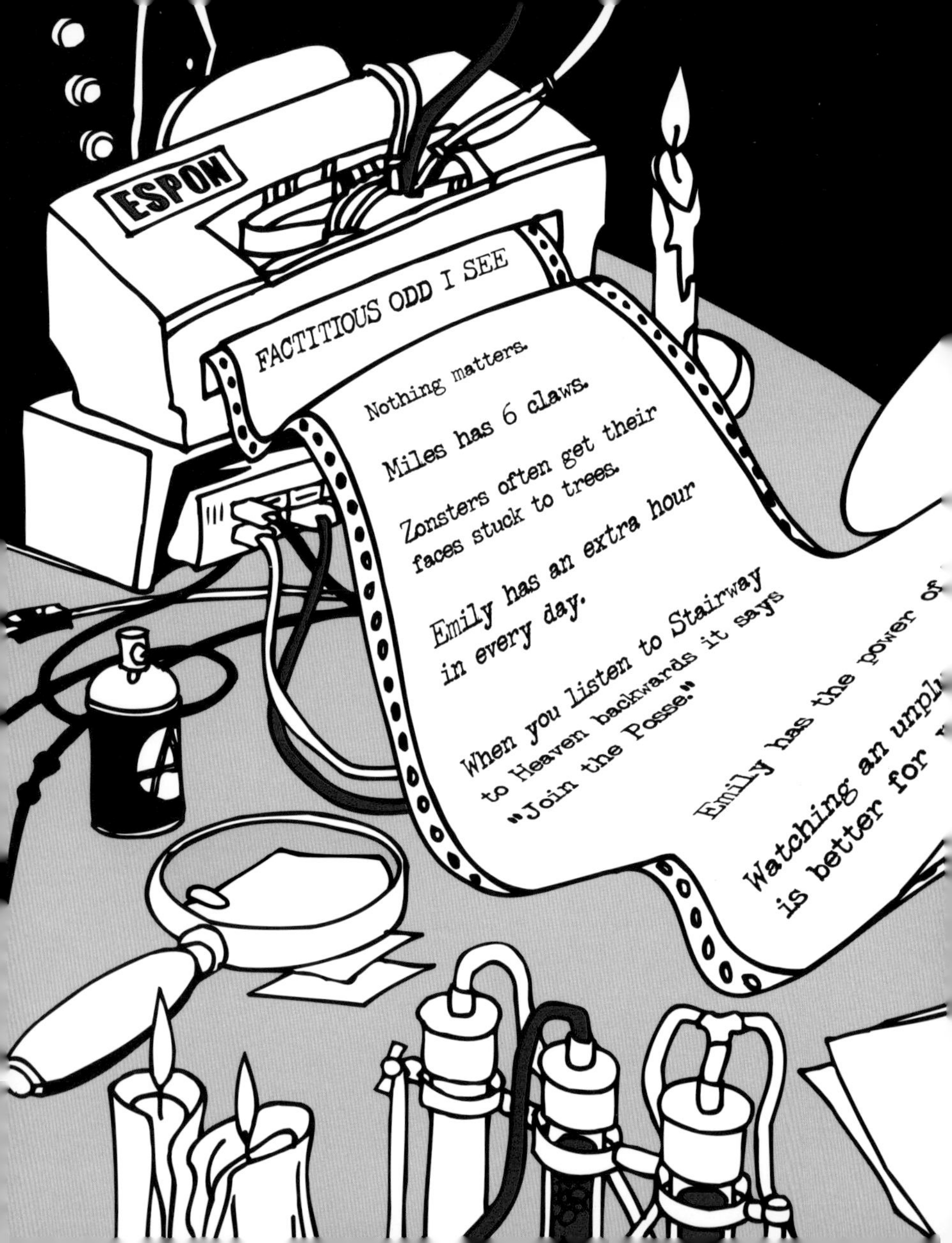
ESPON
FACTITIOUS ODD I SEE
Nothing matters.
Miles has 6 claws.
Zonsters often get their faces stuck to trees.
Emily has an extra hour in every day.
When you listen to Stairway to Heaven backwards it says "Join the Posse."

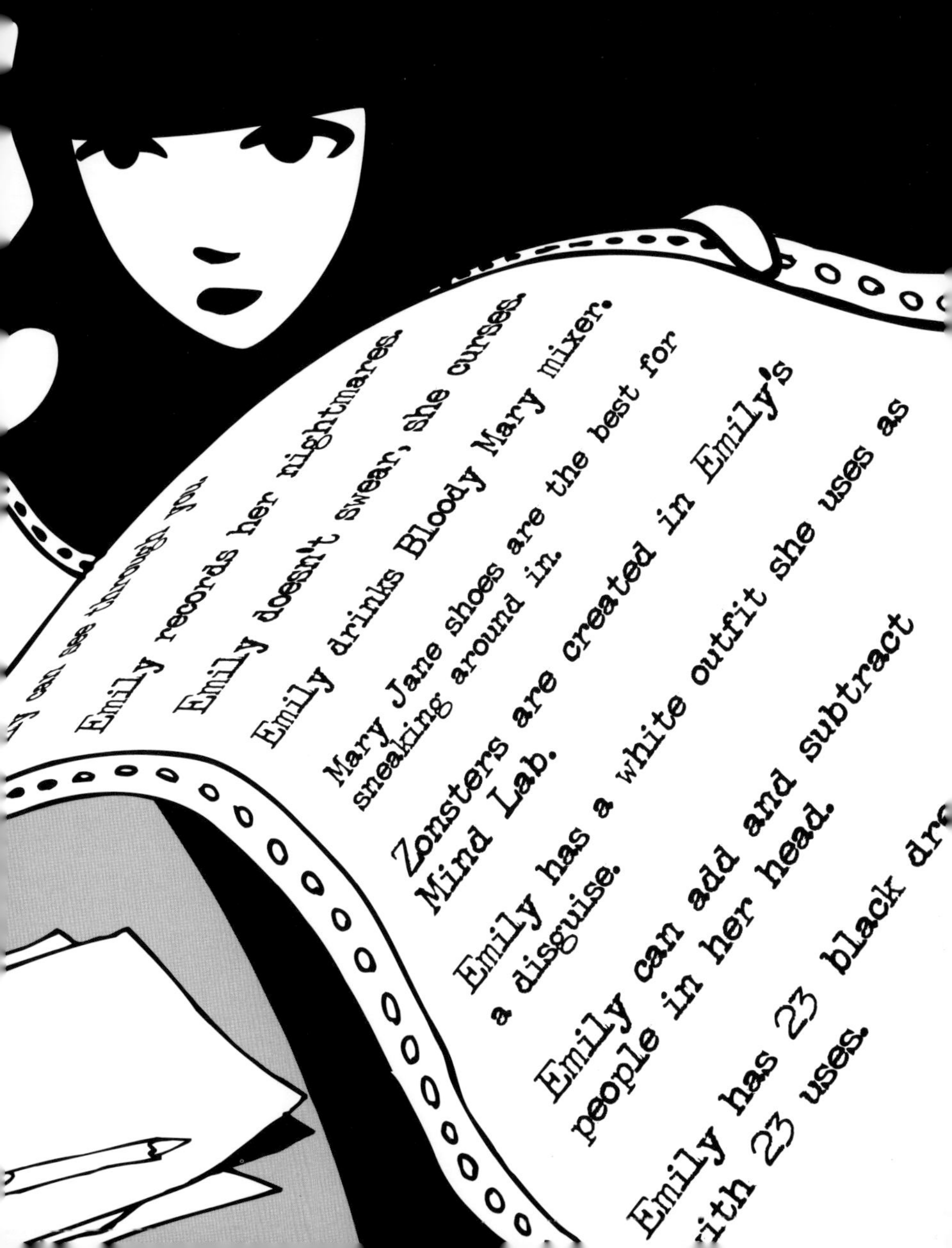

y can see through you.
Emily records her nightmares.
Emily doesn't swear, she curses.
Emily drinks Bloody Mary mixer.
Mary Jane shoes are the best for sneaking around in.
Zonsters are created in Emily's Mind Lab.
Emily has a white outfit she uses as a disguise.
Emily can add and subtract people in her head.
Emily has 23 black dr
ith 23 uses.

BE

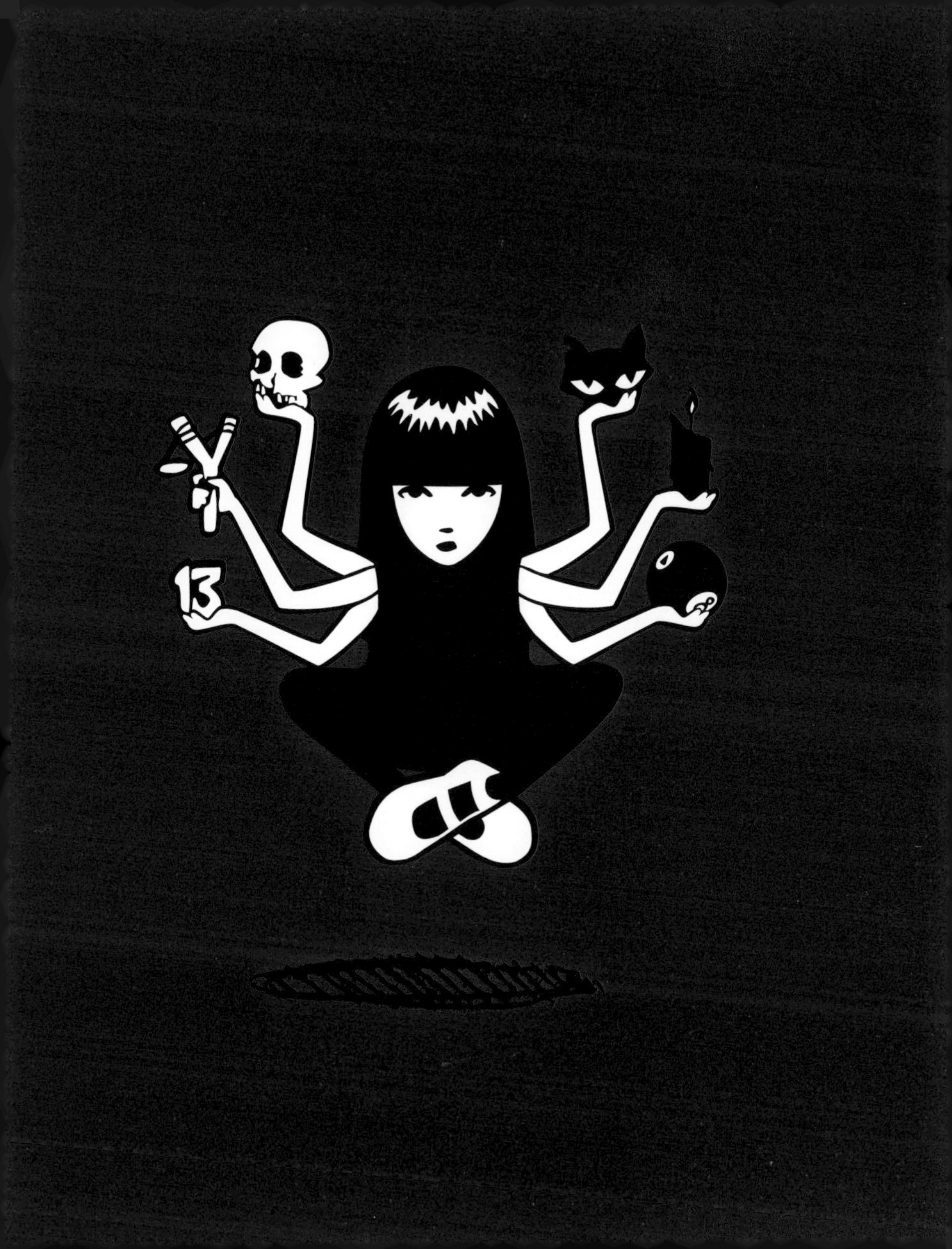
13

Emily isn't scared of monsters...

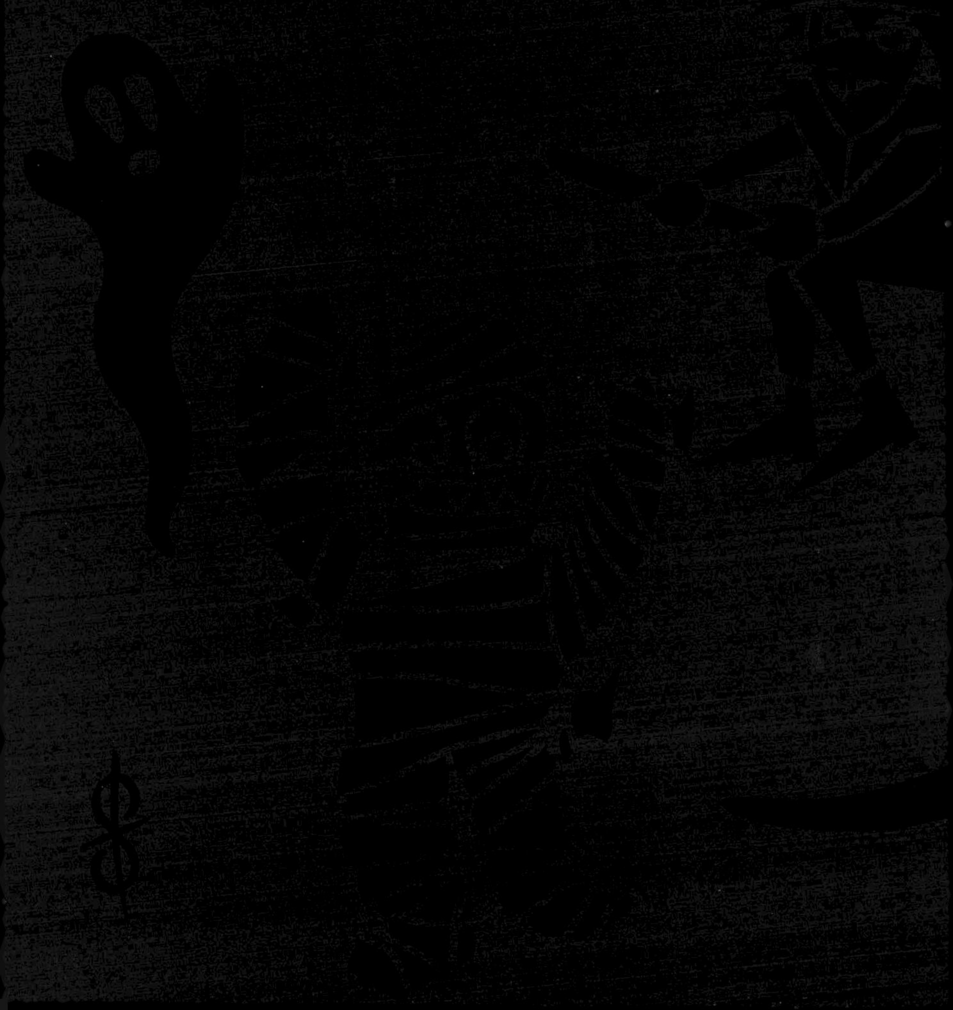

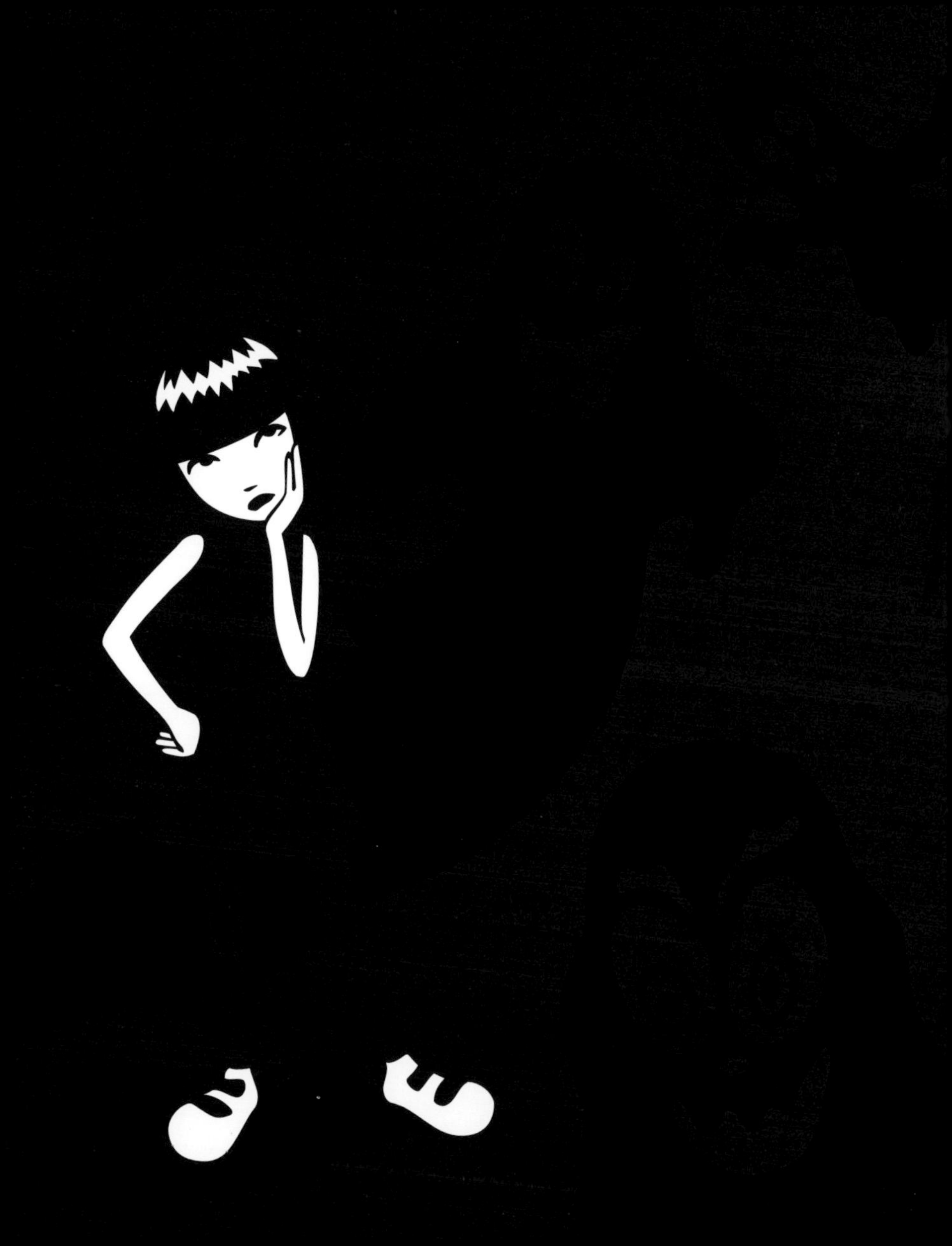

...she creates Zonsters!

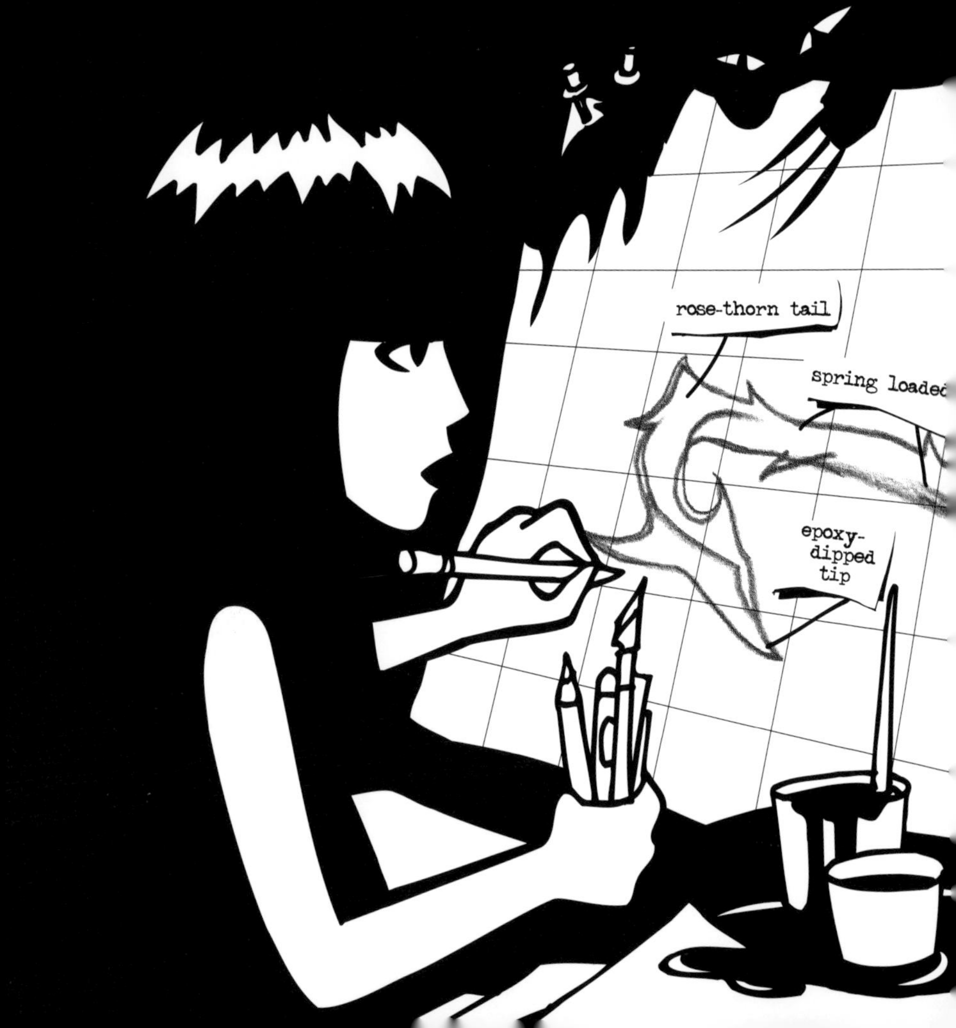
rose-thorn tail
spring loaded
epoxy-dipped tip

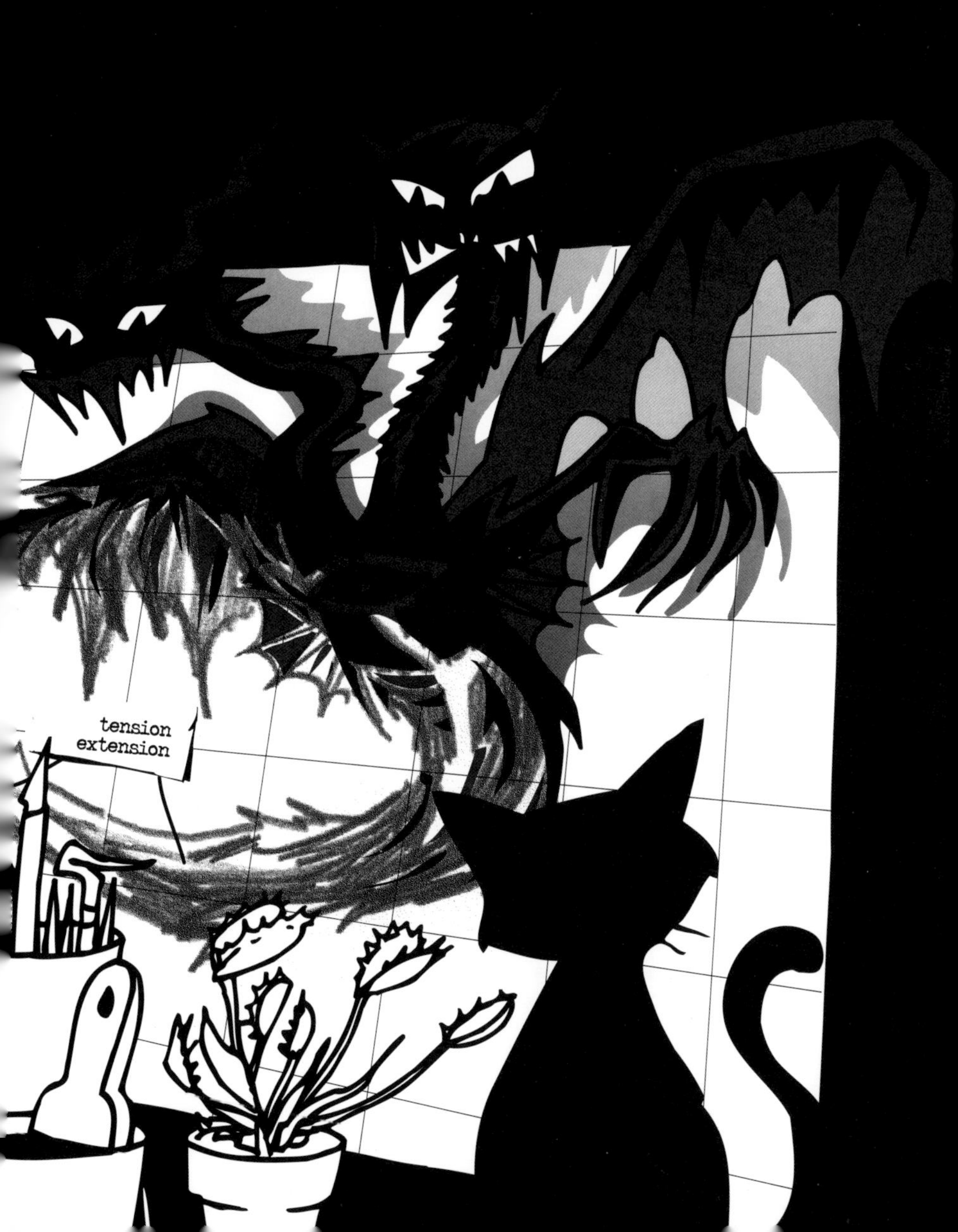
tension
extension

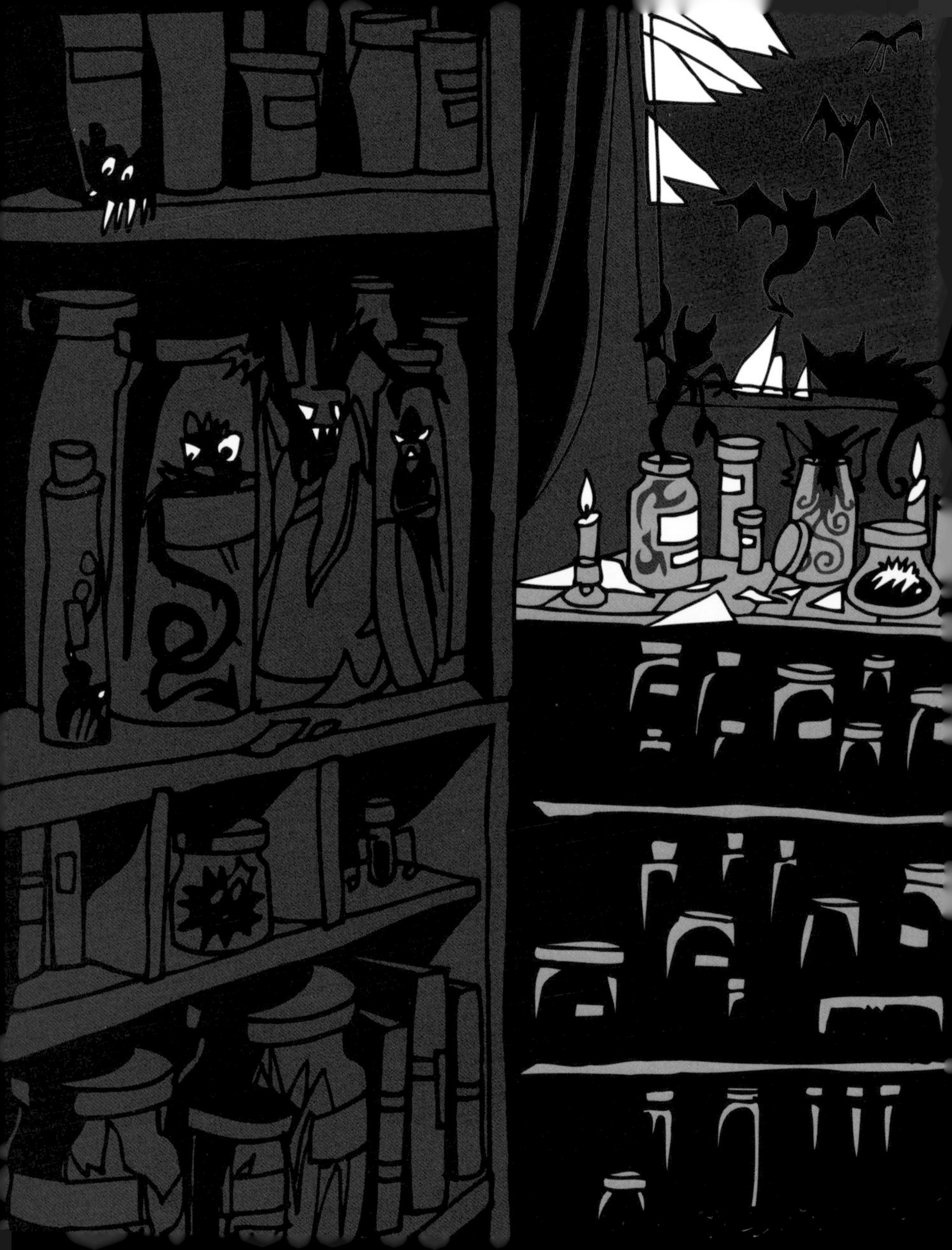

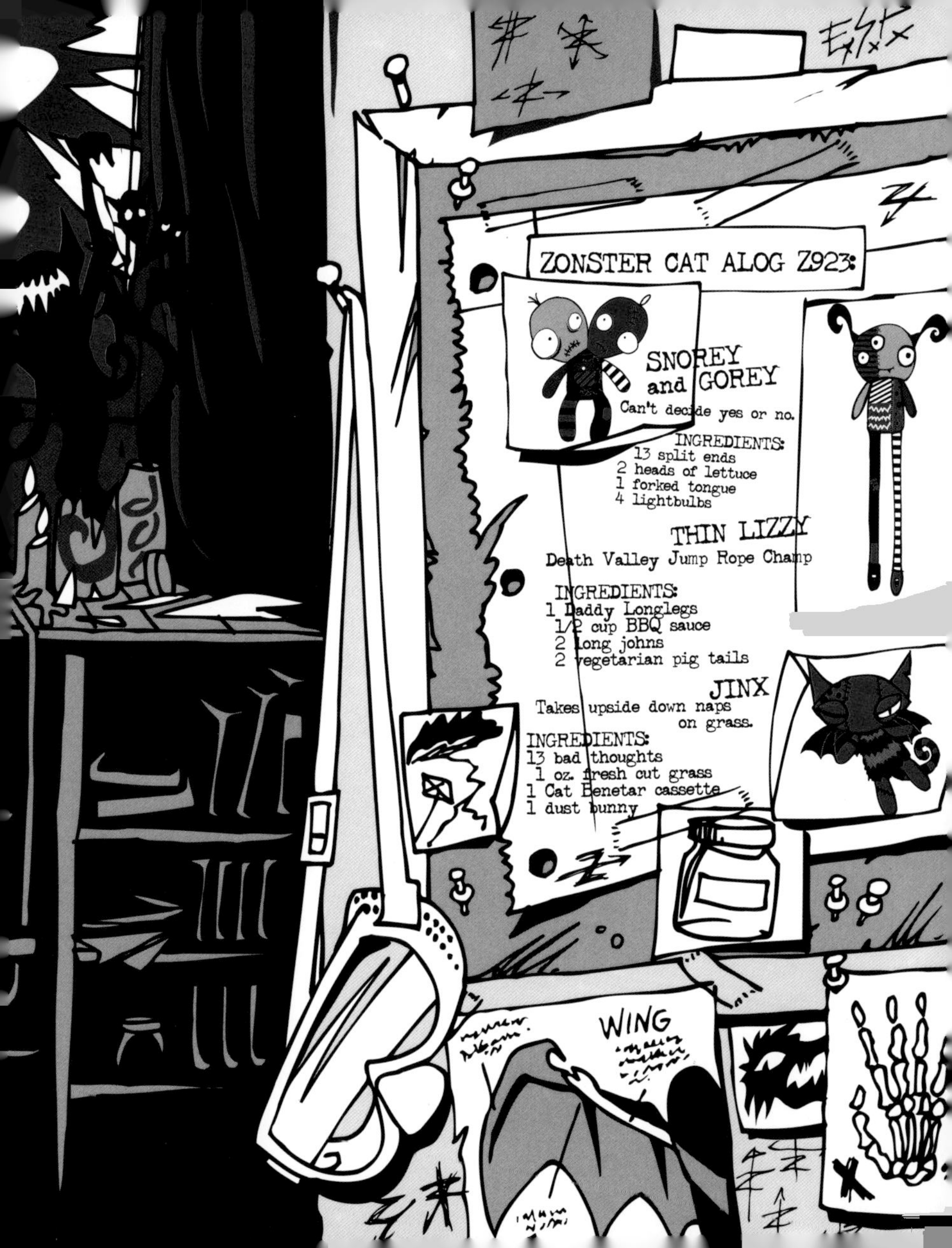
ZONSTER CAT ALOG Z923:
SNOREY and GOREY
Can't decide yes or no.
INGREDIENTS:
13 split ends
2 heads of lettuce
1 forked tongue
4 lightbulbs
THIN LIZZY
Death Valley Jump Rope Champ
INGREDIENTS:
1 Daddy Longlegs
1/2 cup BBQ sauce
2 long johns
2 vegetarian pig tails
JINX
Takes upside down naps on grass.
INGREDIENTS:
13 bad thoughts
1 oz. fresh cut grass
1 Cat Benetar cassette
1 dust bunny
WING

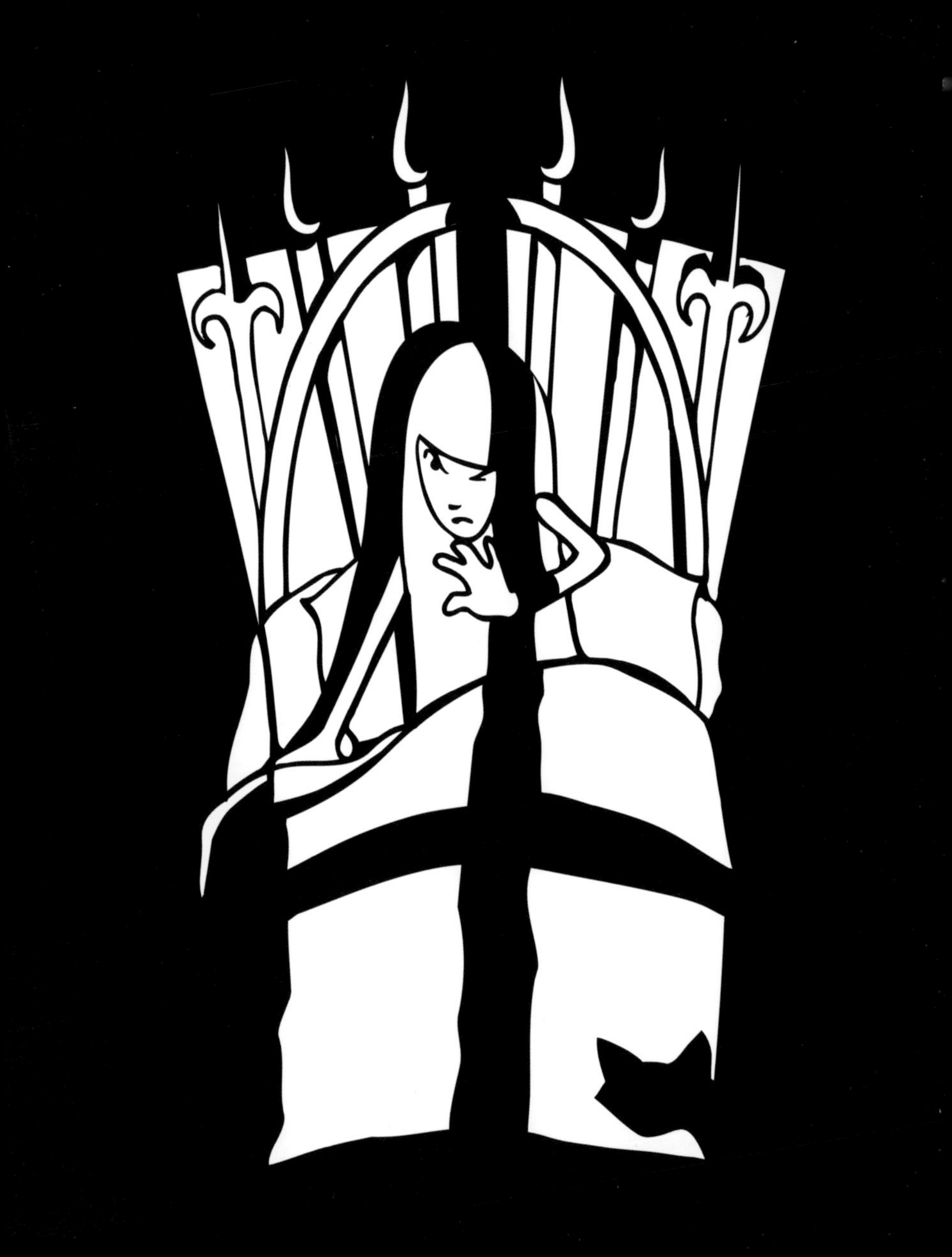

If Emily had her way...

...every day

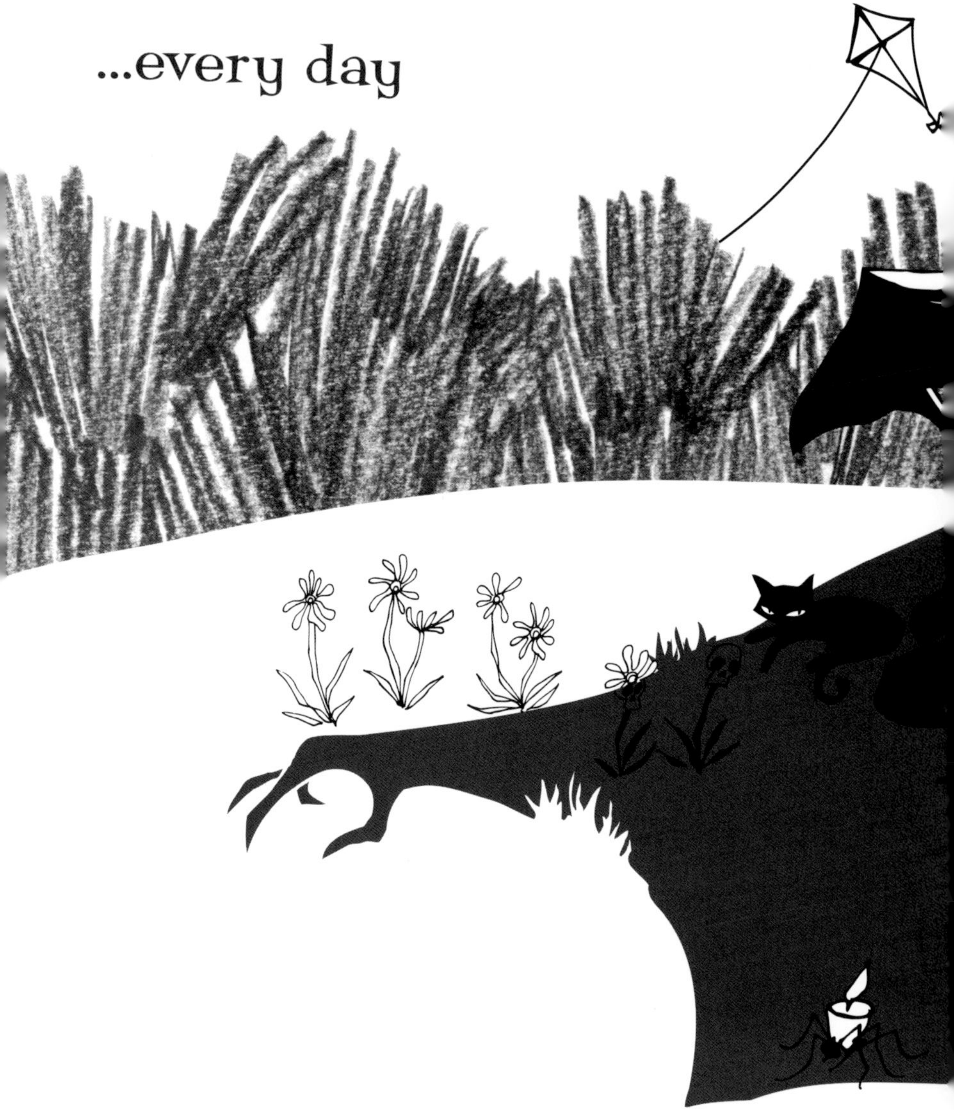

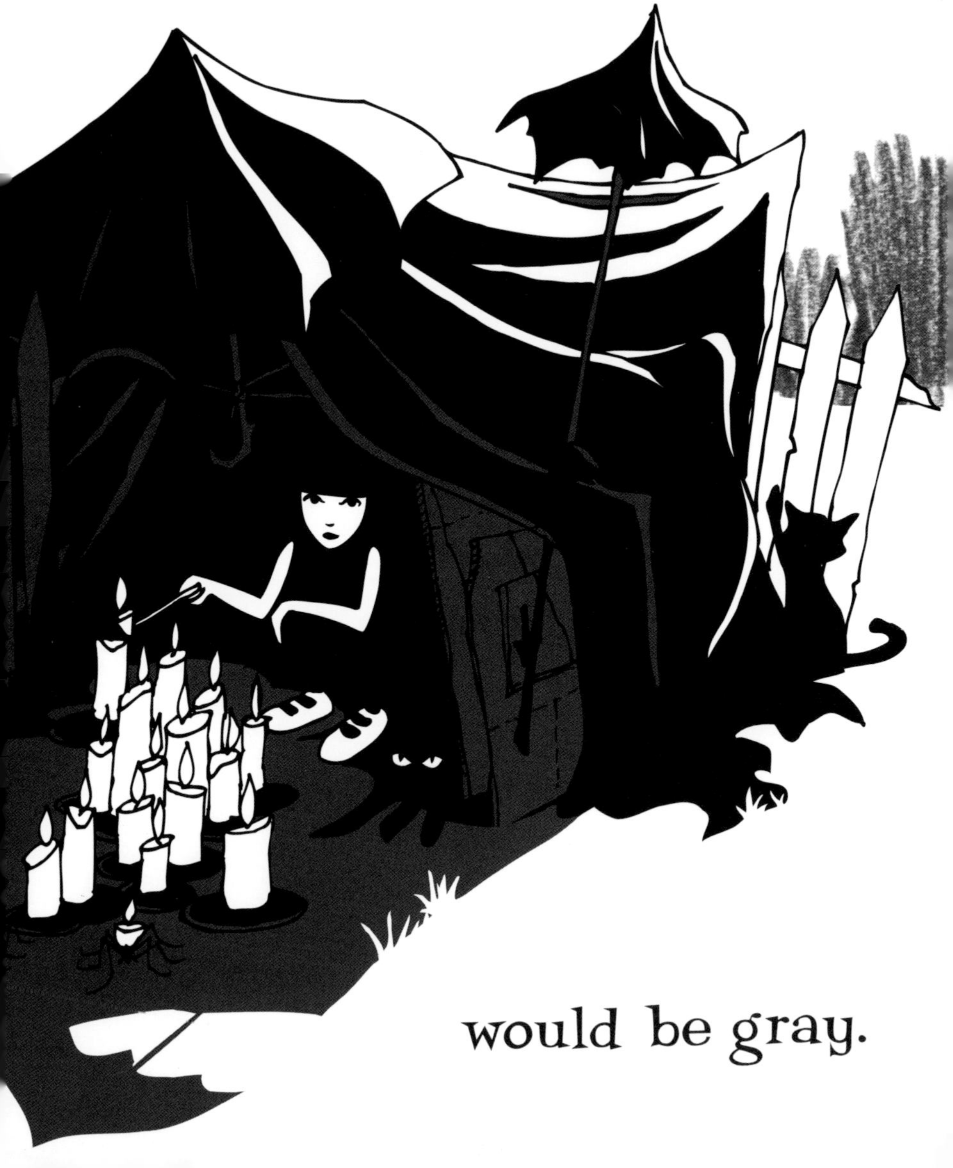

would be gray.

Let there be dark.

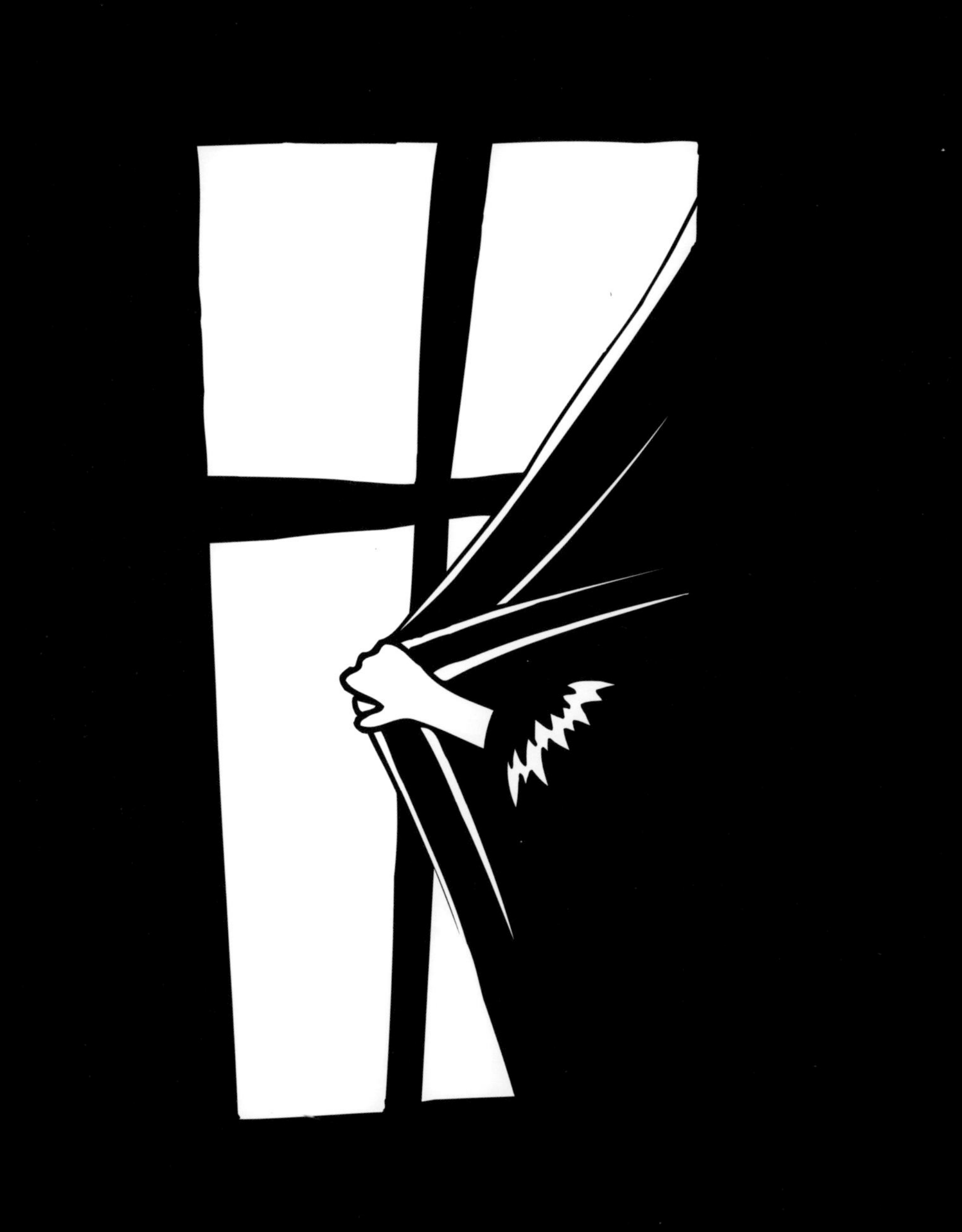

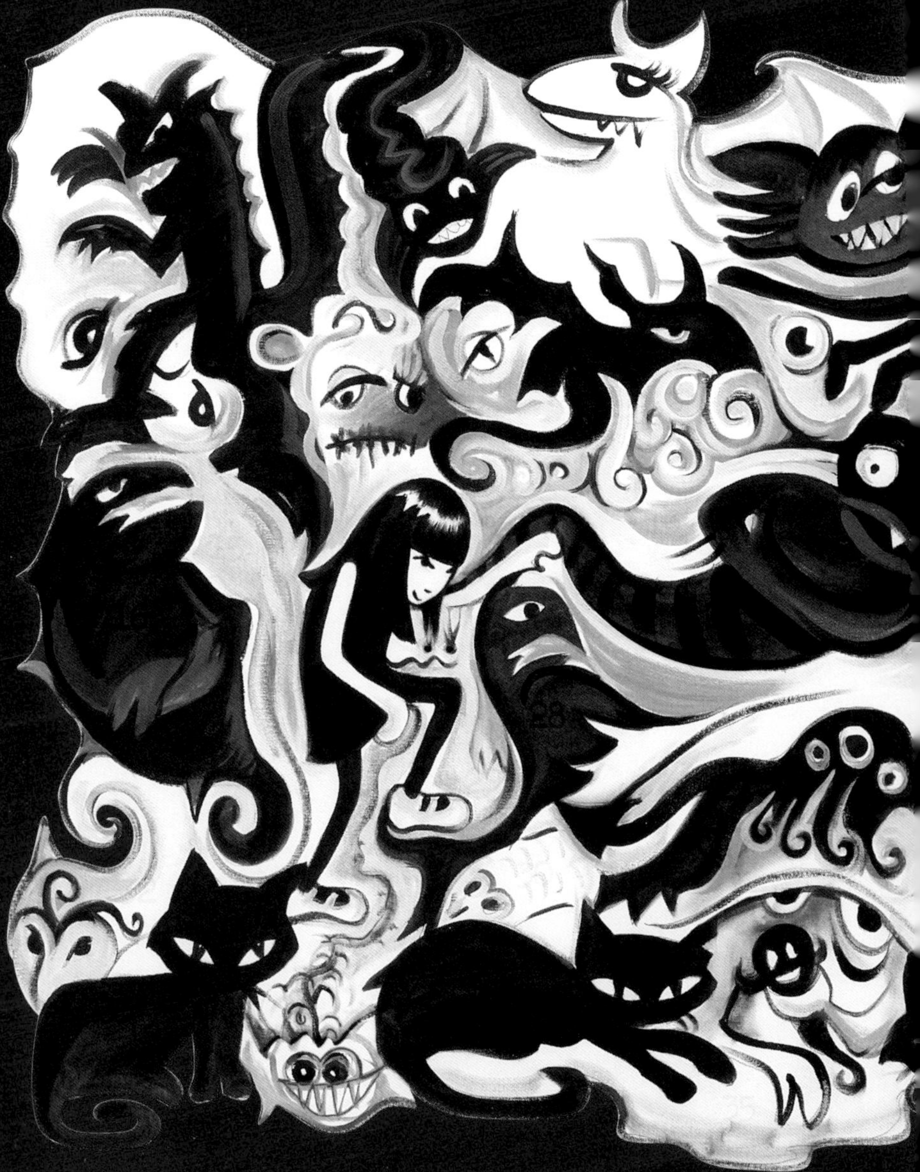

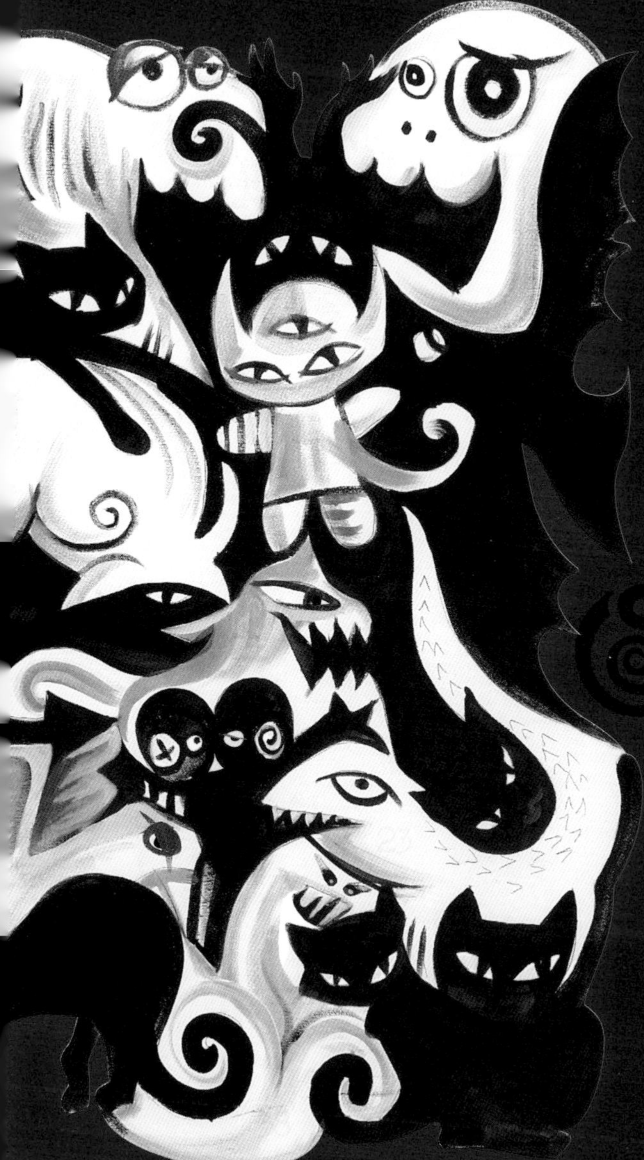

THE FEW THE PROUD THE STRANGE

1 Shanonozon
2 Pillowgoat
3 Lizon
4 Eringzo
5 Zonstacy
6 Leetomazon
7 Zonthorstin
8 Huguru
9 Ogle
10 Grishamizon
11 Adelezon
12 Miles
13 Kerizon
14 Noazon
15 Ubanazon
16 Matmozon
17 Mystery
18 Moonizon
19 el Groopezon
20 Jesickazon
21 Bonnizon
22 Levittizon
23 Re-becazon
24 Zongra Cezon
25 Triazon
26 Buzzonious
27 Boo
28 Zontrasee
29 Mikylazon
30 Mandanazon
31 Vonderzon
32 Beserrazon
33 NeeChee
34 Sabbath
35 Robozon
36 Lupazon
37 Emily
38 Thujazon
39 Gudgle
40 Percy

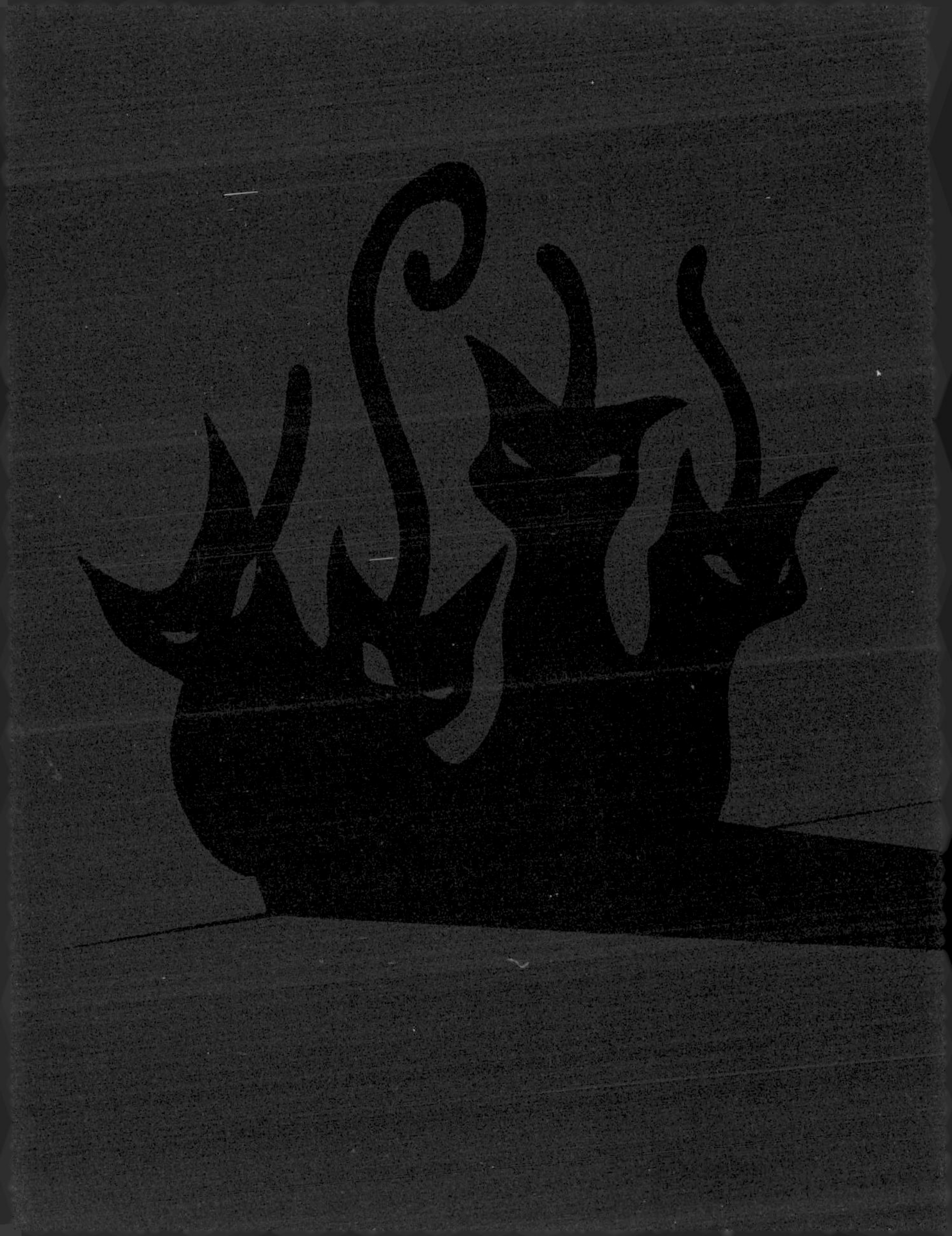

now get strange
or get lost!